Cliffs of Moher, Co. Clare (commons.wikimedia.org)

Ireland, also known as Eire or The Emerald Isle, is the perfect destination for a road trip and there are many reasons why.

Despite the small size of Ireland, with it being just 84,420 sq. kilometres (52,456 sq. miles), you will be pleasantly surprised by the endless opportunities of things to see and do. This small country offers history, a unique culture, and stunning scenery. It can all be discovered at your own leisurely pace, no matter how much time you have.

Our *Ultimate Irish Road Trip Guide* will detail the must-see main attractions, unique hidden gems and top tips so you can get the best out of your Irish adventure.

Contents

Understanding Ireland

Our Rich History

Ireland is a history museum in itself, with many ruins, castles and monuments sprawled out all over the entire island.

The first evidence of people living in Ireland dates back to 8,000 BC when the hunter-gatherers arrived here during the last Ice Age. Since then, there have been many changes, including cultural influences, civil wars, religious reforms, and struggles for independence, which have shaped the country.

The island of Ireland is divided into The Republic of Ireland, which is home to 26 counties, and Northern Ireland, which is part of Great Britain and is home to the remaining six counties. Our road trip guide includes the whole island of Ireland.

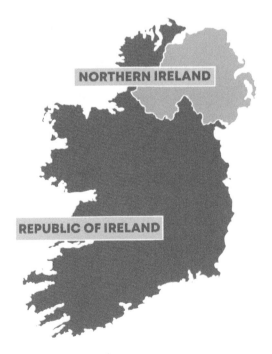

NORTHERN IRELAND

REPUBLIC OF IRELAND

Orientation

One of the main reasons for the division of Ireland was religion. Northern Ireland was predominantly Protestant, and what is now known as The Republic of Ireland, was mostly Catholic. Of course, there were small minorities of the Catholics in the North and Protestants in the South, which in turn led to 'The Troubles' of the 1990s. Some wanted to be part of the United Kingdom, and some wanted a united Ireland. Today, Ireland is very progressive, with many nationalities, ethnicities and religions living side by side in harmony.

Climate

Luckily Ireland does not suffer from the extremes of temperature experienced by many other countries at a similar latitude. The hills and mountains, many of which are near the coastline, provide shelter from strong winds and direct oceanic influence, which means that winters tend to be cool and windy, while summers are mostly mild and less breezy. As the years go on, and with the increase in climate change worldwide, Ireland's climate is also ever-changing.

Famous People

For centuries now, there have been many Irish people who have shared their talents with the world. Many famous Irish names exist throughout the globe, including James Joyce, Oscar Wilde, Bono, Colin Farrell, Van Morrison, Michael Collins, Conor McGregor, Maureen O' Hara, Mary Robinson and who can forget St. Patrick himself, whose day is celebrated globally on 17th March every year. There are, of course, many more famous people from the region and even more with Irish heritage, but it would take a whole other book to mention all of them. Needless to say, Ireland and its heritage are proudly displayed by many around the world.

Climate in Ireland (pixy.org)

Getting Here

Where Can You Start?

Ireland has five international airports - Dublin, Cork, Shannon, Knock and Belfast - so if you are coming from abroad, it's worth checking if you have the option to fly to a closer airport to your starting point. This will, of course, depend on where you are flying from. From almost all of these major airports, you can begin your travels with a rental car.

If you are already in Ireland, you can drive straight to your chosen itinerary's starting point and go from there. However, suppose you plan to take your own vehicle to Ireland via ferry. In that case, you will arrive in either Rosslare, Dublin, Larne or Belfast. From there, you can begin the voyage.

Your Starting Point

Your Irish road trip can be as flexible as you like, but it's important to know the best starting points and how to get there to begin the adventure of a lifetime.

Belfast

Beginning your trip from Belfast is a great option to explore The Causeway Coastal Route or The East coast of Ireland. Getting here couldn't be easier, with many travel options available.

Flights: Belfast has two airports, Belfast International Airport located 21 kilometres (13 miles) northwest of Belfast City centre, and the smaller George Best Belfast City Airport located 5 kilometres (3.1 miles) from Belfast City centre.

Ferry: There are two ferry ports in Northern Ireland offering excellent access to Belfast City and the rest of Northern Ireland and Ireland. Larne Ferry port is located on the east coast of Northern Ireland, and Belfast Port located just outside the city centre.

Flights: Dublin International Airport, located 7 kilometres (4.3 miles) north of Dublin City Centre, is Ireland's main international airport and has scheduled flights from all over the world. Connections can also be made here to other parts of the country.

Train: Irish Rail is the main rail network in Ireland and offers routes to Belfast from all over the country. The main station in the city is Belfast Central Railway Station.

www.irishrail.ie

Bus: There are many options for buses to Belfast from all over the country, with Bus Eireann, Dublin Coach and even Aircoach offering frequent services to Belfast and surroundings.

www.aircoach.ie
www.buseireann.ie
www.dublincoach.ie

Dublin

Flights: Dublin International Airport, located 7 kilometres (4.3 miles) north of Dublin City Centre, is Ireland's main international airport and has scheduled flights from all over the world. Connections can also be made here to other parts of the country.

Ferry: Dublin Port is Ireland's busiest port and is located on Dublin's northeast side. Ferries arrive here from the UK and France regularly, and from the port, it is a short

drive to Dublin City Centre and beyond.

Train: Dublin has three major railway stations, Connolly, Pearse and Heuston stations, all of which have intercity and long-distance connections to all parts of the country.

Bus: Bus Eireann, Aircoach and Dublin Coach, have connections to and from Dublin and its surroundings.

Gap of Dunloe (commons.wikimedia.org)

Shannon

Flights: Shannon International Airport is the third busiest airport in the Republic of Ireland, located in County Clare, halfway between Limerick and Ennis. It has scheduled flights to both Europe and the USA, making it a handy place to fly into to start a road trip for Ireland's west coast.

Train: The closest train stations to Shannon are Limerick and Ennis, both served by Irish Rail.

ww.irishrail.ie

Bus: Bus Eireann and Expressway offer scheduled bus services to and from Shannon Airport.

Cork

Flights: Cork International Airport is the second largest of the three airports in the Republic of Ireland and is located 6.5 kilometres (4 miles) south of Cork City. It has regularly scheduled flights to and from all over Europe.

Travelling by car in Ireland (https://www.geograph.ie/)

Train: Cork Kent Railway Station is located 10 minutes from Cork centre and is served by Irish Rail.

Bus: Cork City Bus Station at Parnell Place is the city's central station and is served by Bus Eireann and Expressway.

Best Ways to Get Around

Rental Car/Own Car

Taking a car around Ireland is a great choice. Most of our main roads are great, and you will find parking almost everywhere you want to visit. Don't be fooled by the M (motorways/highways) and N (national) roads, though. Once you get off the beaten track, you must prepare for narrow, windy and challenging routes, which sometimes may need to be tackled during a heavy downpour. It is essential to take extra caution when going off the main roads, especially on the coast and in and around mountainous areas. Of course, you may have your own car, but if not, there are plenty of rental car companies in the country to choose from.

Campervan

If you have the chance, a campervan is an excellent option for a road trip in Ireland. Ireland is very campervan-friendly, and we have an endless variety of campsites to choose from. Staying at camps is a great way to immerse yourself in the Irish culture and also get insider tips for the area. Whether you are a solo traveller or a family of four, a camper van is available to suit you.

The Park4Night app, listed further on in this guide ('Tips from the locals' section), is great to use if travelling by either campervan or car to find facilities and off the beaten track parking spots.

Motorbike

Travelling around Ireland by motorbike is a fantastic way to feel a sense of freedom, with the wind on your skin and the scenery in reaching distance. If you are a keen biker, you will absolutely love travelling Ireland by motorbike, especially the coastal roads and narrow mountain roads. You have the option to take your own motorbike to Ireland or rent a motorbike from one of the rental agencies listed further on.

Ferries

There are ferries between Cork-Santander (Spain) and Cork-Roscoff (France) with Brittany Ferries. Cork-Santander runs four times per week and is 26 hours, and Cork-Roscoff runs twice a week and is 14 hours.

www.britanny-ferries.ie

Rental Companies

Budget

Budget is a rental company known to many. There are locations in Ireland and Northern Ireland but always enquire about crossing the border as there may be extra fees.

www.budget.ie

Irish Car Rentals

With locations in Dublin, Shannon, Knock, Kerry and Cork airports, this cheap car rental is a handy option to check out, and they have many more locations dotted around the country for extra convenience.

www.irishcarrentals.com

Thrifty

Thrifty is a low-cost subsidiary brand of Hertz and offers excellent value for money. The best thing is they offer the option to pick up and drop off at different locations, which is a great way to keep your itinerary flexible.

www.thrifty.ie

Celtic Rider Motorbike Rentals

Here you can rent a motorbike of your choice, as long as you are over 25 and have a valid motorbike licence. All rentals include fully comprehensive insurance and have many other inclusions as long as you rent for a minimum of three days. The rental company is officially approved by Tourism Ireland and Failte Ireland.

Insider Tip: It is also a time-saver to use a comparison website such as Compare Travel which will get you the best deal.

The Hook Lighthouse, Co. Wexford (commons.wikimedia.org)

Highlights

Now, of course, the options are endless when it comes to planning what you want to see and do. Perhaps you and your fellow road trippers have different interests, so we will make this part easy. For your convenience, we've broken this section down to provide you with inspiration.

History & Heritage

Bru Na Boinne Visitor Centre, County Meath

This heritage area in County Meath is home to one of the world's most important prehistoric landscapes. Older than Stonehenge and The Great Pyramids of Giza, the Newgrange passage tomb dates back to 3200 B.C and was built by Stone Age farmers.

Website: www.heritageireland.ie/visit/places-to-visit

Address: Brú na Bóinne, Glebe, Donore, Co. Meath, A92 EH5C

Kilkenny Castle, County Kilkenny

This 12th-century castle, situated in the middle of Kilkenny City, symbolises Norman occupation in Ireland. It is a popular tourist attraction, not only in the county of Kilkenny but in the whole of Ireland.

Website: www.kilkennycastle.ie

Address: The Parade, Collegepark, Kilkenny, R95 YRK1

Dublin Castle, County Dublin

Dating back to the early 13th-century, this castle has had many years of history, beginning with the Viking era, which keeps history buffs returning time and time again.

Price: From €6

Address: Dame St, Co. Dublin

The Giants Causeway, County Antrim

Located in County Antrim, this incredible result of an ancient volcanic eruption cannot be overlooked on an ultimate Irish road trip. This is an area of about 40,000 basalt columns located on the north coast of Northern Ireland and is a phenomenon you must feast your eyes on.

Website: www.nationaltrust.org.uk/giants-causeway

Address: Bushmills BT57 8SU, Northern Ireland

Blarney Castle, Co. Cork (commons.wikimedia.org)

9

Blarney Stone/Blarney Castle, County Cork

Blarney Castle is one of Ireland's biggest attractions. Almost everyone who visits Ireland wants to add this to their list – purely to kiss the Blarney Stone, which is said to give you 'the gift of the gab'.

Website: www.blarneycastle.ie

Address: Monacnapa, Blarney, Co. Cork, T23 Y59

Dalkey Castle, County Dublin

Experience what life was like in the Middle Ages, with actors who portray it all, during the living history tour. Tours include the early Christian graveyard, 14th-century mini castle and a writers' gallery.

Price: From €8.50

Address: Castle St, Dalkey, Co. Dublin

The Rock of Cashel, County Tipperary

A visit to 'The high king of Irish monuments', which possess the most impressive group of medieval buildings in Ireland, is something that needs to be ticked off the Irish bucket list.

Price: From €8

Address: Moor, Cashel, Co. Tipperary

Trim Castle, County Meath

This castle may look familiar, considering it was the filming location for the blockbuster movie *Braveheart*. The castle itself is very impressive and took thirty years to build.

Price: From €1

Address: Castle St, Trim, Co. Meath

Newgrange, County Meath

This impressive passage tomb dating back to 3200 BC is world-famous for being older than Stonehenge and even The Pyramids of Giza.

Price: From €8

Address: Newgrange, Donore, Co. Meath

Slievemore Deserted Village, County Mayo

Discover the remains of an ancient Irish village deserted on Achill Island.

Address: Bal of Dookinelly (Calvy), Co. Mayo

Waterford Treasures, County Waterford

Three key historical museums located within the Viking Triangle in Waterford City – an absolute must.

Address: Cathedral Square, The Viking Triangle, Co. Waterford

Giants Causeway, Co. Antrim (commons.wikimedia.org)

Visitor Attractions

Cliffs of Moher, County Clare

These impressive cliffs tower 393 feet (120 metres) above the wild Atlantic Ocean and are one of the biggest tourist attractions on the island. Once, the cliff had a path which was unprotected but due to the risk of falling, there is a secondary path further in, so be sure not to be tempted to walk on the old path. Believe it or not, the cliffs have been here for over 350 million years, and are part of the UNESCO global geopark. It is recommended to spend at least two hours here to enjoy the scenery but also to learn about the cliffs at the visitor centre.

Price: From €5

Website: www.cliffsofmoher.ie

Cliffs of Moher, Co. Clare (commons.wikimedia.org)

Trinity College, County Dublin

Trinity College dates back to 1592 and is a popular attraction in the heart of Dublin City. It is particularly famous for housing the Book of Kells. The Trinity Library is most likely one of the most impressive libraries you will ever see with over seven million books and a significant amount of historic manuscripts.

Website: www.tcd.ie

Address: College Green, Dublin 2

Guinness Storehouse, County Dublin

Learn what it takes to pour the ultimate pint of the 'black stuff' at the original Guinness Storehouse in Dublin City. Here you will learn all about the history, the brewing process and you will even get to pour your own pint at the end of the tour. Spend as long as you please chilling in The Gravity Bar, overlooking the city at the very top of the building. Be sure to book tickets in advance.

Price: From €15

Website: www.guinness-storehouse.com

Address: St. James's Gate, Dublin 8, D08 VF8H

Titanic Museum, Belfast City

Take a journey back in time, when the Titanic was ready to set sail. This is the largest Titanic visitor centre in the world, with nine interactive galleries. If you find yourself in Belfast, this is a must-do experience.

Price: From €19

Website: www.titanicbelfast.com

Address: 1 Olympic Way, Queen's Road, Belfast BT3 9EP, United Kingdom

Old Bushmills Distillery, County Antrim

Founded in 1608, this popular tourist attraction has an average of 120,000 visitors per year and should not be missed when in Northern Ireland. It has become one of the most famous Irish whiskeys worldwide.

Price: From €9

Address: 2 Distillery Rd, Bushmills, County Antrim

The English Market, County Cork

Have a wander around this bustling 18th-century market and browse local and organic produce from the region.

Address: Princes St, Centre, Co. Cork

EPIC Museum, County Dublin

This museum is an absolute must if you want to get to know in-depth Irish history in an exciting and interactive setting.

Address: The Chq Building, Unit 32 /33, N Wall Quay, North Wall, Dublin 1, Co. Dublin

Crumlin Road Gaol, County Antrim

Explore this 150-year-old gaol (jail) where seventeen men have been executed. Get to know the history and, more importantly, the secrets of the jail.

Address: 53-55 Crumlin Rd, Belfast, Co. Antrim

Cork City Gaol, County Cork

This restored 19th-century prison is somewhat castle-like and is worth a visit when in Cork City.

Price: From €6

Address: Convent Ave, Sunday's Well, Co. Cork

Kilmainham Gaol, County Dublin

This jail plays a huge role in Irish history, considering many Irish leaders were detained here, and some even executed. A guided tour is recommended and make sure to pre-book.

Price: From €4

Address: Inchicore Rd, Kilmainham, Dublin 8, Co. Dublin

Kilmainham Gaol, Co. Dublin (commons.wikimedia.org)

Blackrock Castle Observatory, County Cork

Science enthusiasts will love this observatory, focusing on all things astronomy.

Price: From € 4.50

Address: Castle Rd, Blackrock, Co. Cork

Jameson Distillery, County Dublin

Take a guided tour of this world famous distillery, including whiskey tastings, history and some cool stories from the expert guides.

Price: From €25

Address: Bow St, Smithfield, Dublin 7, Co. Dublin

Skellig Islands, County Kerry

The Skellig Islands are well known, especially the largest Skellig Michael which was the film location for *Star Wars*. If you're brave enough, walk the cliffside steps to reach the clifftop monastery.

Address: Skellig Rock Great, Cahersiveen, Co. Kerry

Valentia Island, County Kerry

Connected by a land bridge, this island is worth a visit for its magnificent views and real island vibes, with only 665 people living there permanently. Visit the lighthouse and heritage centre.

Address: Cromwell Point, Glanleam, Valentia Island, Co. Kerry

Derry Museum/Siege Museum/ Tower Museum, Count Derry

These museums will give you a great insight into the city of Derry/Londonderry.

Address: 55 Glenfada Park, Co. Derry

Mount Juliet Estate, County Kilkenny

This luxury estate and golf course is a beautiful place to explore. From the serene landscape to spa treatments and Michelin-star dining, Mount Juliet is a place you can well and truly treat yourself.

Address: Thomastown, Co. Kilkenny

Guinness Store House, Co. Dublin (commons.wikimedia.org)

Adare Manor, County Limerick

Set on an 840-acre estate, this Neo-Gothic manor hotel and resort is a sight to behold. Whether you want to take a stroll on the grounds or opt for some fine dining, the choice is yours.

Address: Adare, Co. Limerick

Westport House and Gardens, County Mayo

This estate dating back to the Georgian era, is a beautiful place to explore, including manicured gardens, a mini railway and a lake.

Address: Quay Rd, Westport Demesne, Westport, Co. Mayo

Waterford Crystal Visitor Centre, County Waterford

When in Waterford, why not take a guided factory tour of the famous crystal makers Waterford Crystal, where they also have an in-house store selling their high-end crystal.

Price: From €8

Address: 28 The Mall, Co. Waterford

Lafcadio Hearn Japanese Gardens, County Waterford

An enchanting escape to nature, in the heart of Tramore town, which has a truly inspiring backstory. The concept of the gardens is to lead the visitor from birth to death and from earth to heaven.

Price: From €3

Address: Tramore House, Pond Rd, Tramore East, Tramore, Co. Waterford

Avoca Handweavers, County Wicklow

This is Ireland's oldest working handweaving mill and is definitely worth a visit. Take a tour, browse the handwoven creations and even have a delicious homemade lunch while you are here.

Address: The Mill at Avoca Village, Kilmagig Lower, Avoca, Co. Wicklow

Powerscourt Estate, House and Gardens, County Wicklow

For a date with nature, make sure to stop off at Powerscourt Waterfall in County Wicklow, standing tall at 398 feet (121 metres), and surrounded by wildlife and ancient trees in the spellbinding Powerscourt Estate, House and Gardens.

Address: Powerscourt Estate, Enniskerry, Co. Wicklow

Westport House, Co. Mayo (commons.wikimedia.org)

Game of Thrones Locations

If you are a *GOT* fan, you will know that there are many filming locations in Northern Ireland, so why not make a day of it when in the area? The main areas include Ballintoy Harbour, Downhill Beach, Cushendun Caves and the Glens of Antrim to name but a few.

Adventure

Surfing

We are lucky to have 3,172 kilometres (1,970 miles) of coastline, so there are places to suit beginners and professionals alike. There are 21 surf spots in Ireland with the most popular being in Donegal, Sligo and Kerry.

However, if you find yourself on the east coast of Ireland, Waterford is home to some sweet swells. Some of the reasons people choose Ireland as a prime surf spot are because the offshore conditions are regular, the surfing quality is great and better yet, the waves aren't crowded.

Hiking

If you don't fancy climbing high up, there are countless trails and easy day-long hikes to choose from. If you fancy going a bit further, then there are many long-distance excursions and walks too, including The Kerry Way and The Wicklow Way.
When in Glendalough, we recommend hiking the easy and very rewarding trail known as The Spinc. Just follow the signs from the car park in Glendalough and be sure to get a map from the visitor centre (moderate).

Carrauntoohil, County Kerry is Ireland's highest mountain at 3,408 feet (1039 metres). You can reach the top between four to six hours, depending on your fitness level. This is best done on a dry, non-windy day (moderate to challenging).

Croagh Patrick in County Mayo stands tall at 2,506 feet (764 metres) high and can be hiked within three to four hours. The views over Clew Bay and the islands are incredible, so pick a dry, sunny day to enjoy the experience (moderate).

Sea Kayaking

Kayak into darkness in West Cork with Atlantic Sea Kayaking – an experience of a lifetime that has also been mentioned as one of the world's most magical experiences by *The Irish Times*. Not only will you get to see the majestic West Cork coastline from the open sea, but you will also get to know the history of Ireland and meet like-minded individuals.

Surfing in Ireland (pixabay.com)

Mountain Biking

See Ireland from the trails. Ballyhoura, shared by counties Cork and Limerick, has the largest trail network of its kind in the country, combined with a drop-dead gorgeous backdrop, so it's the perfect place to start your Irish biking adventure. As well as Ballyhoura, there are many mountain biking trails all over the country, providing thrills to bike enthusiasts.

Ireland's maritime climate means that mountain biking is an adventure you can take on almost any time of the year. Some of the best spots are Portumna (County Galway), Ballinastoe (County Wicklow), Ticknock (County Dublin) and Clogheen Loop (County Tipperary).

Sea kayaking in Ireland (commons.wikimedia.org)

Rock Climbing

The east and northeast of Ireland have some of the best and most impressive rock-climbing locations in Europe. Dalkey Quarry, which is only 30 minutes from Dublin , has over 300 routes. The Mourne Mountains, Glendalough and Fairhead are excellent choices too. Check out Discover Ireland and Discover Northern Ireland for more information on what to do in both Northern Ireland and the Republic of Ireland.

Arts & Entertainment

Bord Gais Energy Theatre, County Dublin

This performing arts theatre is where you can catch all the latest shows in Dublin, down at the bustling Dublin docklands. See shows such as *Dirty Dancing*, *The Book of Mormon*, *Waitress* and many other musicals and concerts.

Price: From €21

Website: www.bordgaisenergytheatre.ie

Address: Grand Canal Square, Docklands, Dublin

Music Festivals

Held throughout the year, there is a range of amazing music festivals to check out, suited to all music lovers and set in various parts of the country. A must if you find yourself in Ireland – specifically during the summer periods. Some great festivals we recommend checking out include:

Life Festival: the last weekend in May
Forbidden Fruit: the first weekend in June
Sea Sessions: the third weekend in June
All Together Now: the last weekend in July
Electric Picnic: the first weekend in September

Abbey Theatre, County Dublin

Opened in 1904, Ireland's national theatre hosts various shows in English and in Irish as well as offering various ticket offers and free first previews.

Price: From €10

Website: www.abbeytheatre.ie

Address: 26/27 Abbey Street Lower, North City, Dublin 1, D01 K0F1

Lisdoonvarna Matchmaking Festival, County Clare

This is the biggest of its kind in all of Europe, and it has a long-standing tradition, originally set up to help shy farmers find a wife. Now it is a must-see month-long event each September with music, dancing and endless opportunities to meet a special someone.

Website: www.matchmakerireland.com/

Address: Main St, Rathbaun, Lisdoonvarna, Co. Clare, V95 RY61

Lisdoonvarna Matchmaking Festival, Co. Clare (geograph.ie)

Galway Arts Festival, County Galway

Galway Arts Festival (GIAF) is a major cultural organisation which produces one of Europe's leading international arts festivals and is attended by many people each year. It takes place in the last two weeks of July, so if you are a fan of theatre, music, visual arts, opera, dance, street performance and comedy, this should be added to your itinerary.

Website: https://www.giaf.ie/

Cycle Trails and Bike Hire

Great Western Greenway

This 42 kilometres (26 miles) off-road cycling and walking route is the longest in Ireland and follows the renowned Achill to Westport railway.

Website: www.greenway.ie/

Wild Atlantic Way Cycle Route

2,500 kilometres (1,553 miles) of coast to explore from County Cork to County Donegal along the Wild Atlantic Way. Choose how long or how little you want to cycle.

Website: www.thewildatlanticway.com/route-stages

Ring of Kerry

This 200 kilometres (124 miles) driving and cycling route is an absolute must when in the region.

Website: www.discoverireland.ie/ring-of-kerry

Causeway Coastal Route

Stretching from Castlerock to the Giants Causeway, this 33 kilometres (21 miles) cycle route takes in some breathtaking scenery of the north coast of the island.

Walking and Hiking Trails

The Kerry Way, County Kerry

At over 200 kilometres (124 miles), the Kerry Way is one of Ireland's longest signposted walking trails and one of the most popular. You can do the entire stretch or just a section, as you please.

The Wicklow Way, County Wicklow

The Wicklow Way is a 131 kilometres (81 miles) trail that crosses the majestic Wicklow Mountains in Ireland. It runs from Marlay Park in South Dublin through County Wicklow and ends in County Carlow.

Croagh Patrick, County Mayo

This 2,506 feet (764 metres) high mountain close to Westport, County Mayo, which is a famed pilgrimage site in the country, has unsurpassed views over the west coast and its islands.

Carrauntoohil, County Kerry

Ireland's highest mountain, Carrauntoohill, stands at 3,408 feet (1,039 metres). Carrauntoohil is part of the MacGillycuddy's Reeks mountain range. It is an extremely rewarding climb, and provides great bragging rights as you can tell people you have climbed Ireland's highest mountain.

Heritage Trails

Moneymore Heritage Trail, County Tyrone

There are 17 historic points of interest along this heritage trail, through a settlement over 400 years old.

The Heritage Trail of Glengarriff, County Cork

People have lived in this popular town since the Bronze Age, and there are many points of interest along this trail.

Causeway Coastal Cycle Route (geograph.ie)

Meath Heritage Trail, County Meath

Starting at Tara and finishing at the Battle of the Boyne site, this trail takes in all the heritage areas of the county including Kells, Trim Castle and The Hill of Tara.

Health and Wellness

As well as there being many spa and wellness resorts dotted around the country, there are many opportunities to visit various yoga studios and gyms to keep yourself healthy and mindful during your road trip.

Gyms

Anytime Fitness

Anytime Fitness has two locations in Belfast, three in Dublin and one in Cork. The best thing about these gyms is that they are open 24 hours, making them easy to access all day long. This is ideal for people travelling around Ireland, who usually have a dedicated fitness routine, and can opt for a gym pass on the go.

Contact: +353 (0) 6972471

Ben Dunne Gyms

With locations all over Dublin as well as in Laois, Meath and Waterford, Ben Dunne Gyms is a good option for anyone doing road trips around Ireland's Ancient East, who wants to hit the gym en route. If you are listening to Irish radio as you navigate the roads, you'll be sure to get familiar with the infamous Ben Dunne adverts.

Contact: +353 (0) 6210000

Flye Fit

This is a popular low-cost gym in Dublin and Cork, which is perfect for keeping fit on the road on a budget. They have a total of sixteen gyms, with plenty of classes to choose from so if you are in the area and want a good workout, this is a great option to go for.

Contact: memberservice@flyefit.ie

Health Resorts

Monart Spa, County Wexford

Ireland's only destination spa is a fantastic treat if you find yourself in need of some relaxation while touring the island. It has a Finnish sauna, salt grotto, fifteen treatment rooms, a hydrotherapy pool and an infrared pro suite. Monart Spa even has light and dark relaxation rooms, so you can chill after your treatments and re-energise yourself.

Address: Monart, The Still, Co. Wexford

Work out in Ireland's top gyms (https://unsplash.com/)

Powerscourt Springs, County Wicklow

Ireland's first health farm is an adult-only getaway with a difference. Located on 38 acres of private estate, only thirty minutes from Dublin, this is a retreat away from all the hustle and bustle which offers various spa treatments, guided meditation and yoga surrounded by beautiful scenery.

Website: www.powerscourtsprings.ie

Address: Waterfall Road, Coolakay, Enniskerry, Co. Wicklow, A98 PR62

Voya Seaweed Baths, Co. Sligo (Tourism Ireland)

Voya Seaweed Baths, County Sligo

Taking a break at the Voya Seaweed Baths is a truly Irish experience, and we recommend you try this when on the west coast. The seaweed used for the therapy is hand-harvested from the Atlantic Ocean and is full of health benefits at this bathhouse.

Website: www.voyaseaweedbaths.com

Address: 1 Cannon View, Carrowbunnaun, Strandhill, Co. Sligo, F91 XT44

Farnham Estate Health Spa, County Cavan

This fabulous estate is one of Ireland's favourite spa and wellness destinations, with an array of treatments available using ESPA and Yon-Ka products. The spa is set within the Farnham Estate, which is surrounded by the rolling countryside.

Website: www.farnhamestate.ie

Address: Coras Point, Cavan

Yoga

Burren Yoga Retreats, County Galway

If you fancy something unique and energising, head to The Burren for some yoga and wellness. Retreats can include yoga classes, guided meditations, cooking classes, stunning walks and scenic drives, and a location to die for. The centre is close to the Aillwee Caves and the Cliffs of Moher.

Address: Burren Yoga Retreat Centre, Normangrove, Cappaghmore, Co. Galway, H91 KN72

Cliffs of Moher Retreat

Take a break here to stretch the body and relax the mind while being surrounded by lush natural Irish countryside, including the rugged Cliffs of Moher.

Website: www.cliffsofmoherretreat.com

Address: Moher Lodge, Kinielty, Liscannor, Co. Clare

Wild Atlantic Way Yoga, County Cork

Yoga in an idyllic setting, this yoga sanctuary is located in Kinsale, County Cork, Wild Atlantic Way Yoga is the perfect choice if you are looking for unique experiences, ocean views, plant-based food and inspiring teachers. Not to be missed if you are in this beautiful area.

Website: www.wildatlanticwayyoga.com

Address: Moher Lodge, Kinielty, Liscannor, Co. Clare

Equestrian Centres

If you are into all things equestrian, then these are some great Equestrian Centres in Ireland that you should check out. What better way to see Ireland than from the back of a sturdy Connemara pony or Irish sport horse.

Ashford Equestrian Centre, County Galway

Boasting beautiful scenes, this centre is in an idyllic location, nestled between Lough Corrib and Lough Mask, and offers riding lessons to complete beginners, families with young children and experienced riders, so there's something for everyone. It is open seven days a week, and there are additional activities that you can do, apart from horse ridings, such as archery, kayaking, and water skiing.

Website: www.ashfordoutdoors.com

Address: Ashford, Cong, Co. Galway

Eagle Rock Equestrian Centre, County Kerry

Take on some stunning beach and mountain treks during your visit to Eagle Rock Equestrian Centre. Suppose you are more of an experienced rider. In that case, you can venture off onto one of the many trails, which will provide incredible views of the surrounding areas.

Website: www.discoverireland.ie/kerry/eagle-rock-equestrian-centre

Address: Ballycarnahan, Caherdaniel, Co. Kerry

Croagh Patrick Co. Mayo (commons.wikimedia.org)

Gransha Equestrian Centre, County Down

If you are in Northern Ireland, stop by Gransha Equestrian Centre in Bangor. Just a half an hour's drive from Belfast and perfect for young children, rest assured this is a perfect option for their first riding lessons. Lessons are taught to kids from age five upwards.

Website: www.granshaequestrian.com

Address: 10A Kerrs Rd, Bangor BT19 7QD, United Kingdom

Donegal Equestrian Centre, County Donegal

With beach camps, pony rides and riding lessons available at this centre in the seaside town of Bundoran, it would be a shame not to stop and see what all the fuss is about. Many itineraries pass through Donegal – Bundoran in particular. Given that this is one of the most beautiful stretches of coastline in Ireland, we urge you to see it from a different perspective: by horseback.

Website: www.donegalequetriancentre.com

Address: Finner Rd, Finner, Bundoran, Co. Donegal

Tourist Information Centres

Of course, what is travelling without a trip to a tourist information centre? You may have planned your whole route, but there will always be something new you can learn from the locals in the various tourist offices. These are great places to ask any questions you may have and get your bearings. Offering maps and brochures, you may even find out the best places for food and drinks. Tip: many tourist information centres will have free WiFi, too, so if you need to download an online map, check your emails or upload a couple of holiday snaps, this can be a great pitstop.

Belfast Welcome Centre

Address: Belfast Welcome Centre, 47 Donegall Pl, Belfast BT1 5AD, United Kingdom

Connemara Visitor Information Centre

Address: Letterfrack, Co. Galway

Donegal Equestrian Centre, Co. Donegal

Cork City Tourist Information Centre

Address: Cork Tourist Information Centre, 125 St Patrick's St, Centre, Cork, T12 AE81

Tourist Information Centre, Dublin City

Address: 17 O'Connell Street Lower, North City, Dublin, D01

Hidden Gems of Ireland

Sure isn't this what we are all looking for? Ireland has a huge variety of hidden gems. Still, you will more than likely find some yourself that are not listed here because, let's face it, the possibilities are endless.

Our hidden gems consist of beautiful beaches, museums, breweries and epic scenery. Remember to keep your eyes open on your Irish adventure because you will more than likely spot a sign or two, taking you off the beaten track to some more.

Sally Gap, County Wicklow

There are many 'gaps' in Ireland that provide outstanding scenery, including Molls Gap and Gap of Dunloe. These will most certainly be on your route when doing the Ring of Kerry. When in and around the Wicklow Mountains, however, Sally Gap must be explored. Be aware if you have a big vehicle – this will be a tricky drive. However, it is entirely doable if you take your time and allow plenty of space for oncoming traffic.

Address: Sheephaven Bay, Co. Donegal

Belfast Welcome Centre, Co. Antrim

Museum of Country Life, County Mayo

As many road trips pass through Castlebar (County Mayo), we highly recommend stopping here to check out the free museum that documents travellers' lives in rural Ireland. This centre will offer insight into Irish people throughout the ages. It will also show you how different life was for the islanders living off the mainland.

Address: Turlough Park House, Gortnafolla, Castlebar, Co. Mayo, F23 HY31

Murder Hole Beach, County Donegal

This beach is quite off the beaten track but worth it in the end. You won't be able to drive here, but once parked, it is only a short hike until you reach the beach. It is situated on the Melmore Head Peninsula and is actually called Boyeeghter Strand (just in case you see signs with this name, you'll know why). The beach is beautiful, but don't be fooled: swimming here is not recommended due to the strong currents.

Address: Sheephaven Bay, Co. Donegal

Murder Hole Beach, Co. Donegal (tourismireland.com)

Franciscan Well Brewery, County Cork

Irish people love beer. People around the world love Irish beer. So, when in Ireland you need to try out some of the local beer, and this is one brewery that is particularly unique. Home of craft beer in Cork City, serving signature cocktails, spirits, a range of craft beers, and brewery tours is the Franciscan Well Brewery. The brewery is built on the site of a medieval monastery, hence the name, and it even has a pizzeria which sources every single ingredient locally and mills its own flour on-site. Along with Killarney Brewing Company in Killarney and Rascals Brewing in Dublin, this is an essential attraction, if you are a lover of beer.

Address: 14 N Mall, Sunday's Well, Cork, T23 P264

Victors Way, County Wicklow

A sculpture park like no other located near Roundwood, this is an idyllic detour on your way to Glendalough. Victors Way is a unique, privately-owned meditation garden. It is a place of reflection and silence, so bringing children is not encouraged. It has various Indian granite sculptures, a few small lakes, forested areas, and the opportunity to try 'forest bathing'.

Address: Mullinaveige, Co. Wicklow

Japanese Gardens, County Kildare

Gardens to symbolize a soul from oblivion to eternity, these awe-inspiring gardens were created between 1906 and 1910 and represent a soul's journey from oblivion to eternity. They are regarded as one of the finest Japanese gardens in Europe, and over one hundred thousand guests visit every year.

Address: Brallistown Little, Tully, Co. Kildare, R51 KX25

Wildlife

Phoenix Park

Being one of the largest enclosed parks in any European city, it's no wonder the deer absolutely thrive here. The 707 hectares park is enclosed behind 11 kilometres (6.8 miles) of park wall and has been home to deer since the 17th-century. They can be seen all the time, and considering the park has a main road running through it, it goes without saying that you should drive slowly when in the park

Address: Dublin 8

Saltee Islands

One of the best sea bird sanctuaries in Europe. Lying 5 kilometres (3.1 miles) off County Wexford, the two Saltee Islands (Great Saltee and Little Saltee) have been unoccupied since the 20th-century and are now privately-owned. The large island is the most famous bird sanctuary in Ireland, and permission is not needed to visit it. There is a ferry from Kilmore Quay if you don't have your own boat.

Address: Kilmore Quay

Wild Atlantic Way

This entire stretch of west coast (2,500 kilometres/1,553 miles) is not only wild and windswept with undeniable vistas, but the longest defined coastal route in the world. It is home to a variety of wildlife, which you may even spot from your car window if you are lucky. You will have the opportunity to feast your eyes on all types of marine life along the coast and even more so if you get out on the water, be that by ferry, kayak or even surfing.

Address: West Ireland

Japanese Gardens, Co. Kildare (tourismireland.com)

Fota Wildlife Park

This zoo for endangered animals is located on Fota Island in County Cork. It is home to nearly thirty mammals and fifty bird species. Lemurs and wallabies roam freely with the visitors, while larger animals such as giraffes and bison are in habitats. There are also red pandas, tapirs, siamang gibbons amongst many other animals.

Address: Fota Wildlife Park, Fota, Carrigtohill, Co. Cork

The Wexford Wildfowl Reserve

Situated just 8 kilometres (5 miles) outside of Wexford town, this National Nature Reserve is a place that is popular with photographers, tourists, locals and nature lovers. You can see cuckoos, mute swans, whooper swans, mallard ducks, lapwings, and the Greenland geese that migrate here for winter. Bird lovers will be in their element.

Address: Ardcavan, North Slob, Co. Wexford, Y35 EY8

Top Restaurants

Yes, Ireland is famous for its hearty and delicious cuisine, and we know how hard it can be to choose a place to eat, when there are so many options, so we have broken it down for you, by province and by your culinary preference.

Ulster

Fisk Seafood Bar, County Donegal

If you want some of the freshest seafood in Ireland, complete with a stunning view over Sheephaven Bay, then Fisk Seafood Bar cannot be missed. Choose from a delicious menu that includes dishes such as spiced butter prawns, fish tacos, crab claws and Donegal oysters.

Address: The Harbour Bar, Downings, Co. Donegal, F92XR53, F92 XR53

McGarrigles, County Donegal

If you are looking for high-quality food at prices to suit all budgets, you need to try McGarrigles.

Address: Main St, Drumacrin, Bundoran, Co. Donegal

The Shipquay Restaurant, Count Derry

For all your food needs, seven days a week, they offer brunch, lunch or a quick bite to eat in the perfect location of Derry City. Close to the shopping and arts district.

Address: 15-17 Shipquay St, Co. Derry

Fisk Seafood Bar , Co. Donegal

The Lantern Restaurant, County Antrim

A fantastic bistro in the heart of the city, head here if you're looking for a varied menu with locally sourced Northern Irish ingredients.

Address: 58 Wellington Pl, Belfast, Co. Antrim

McNean House and Restaurant, County Cavan

This restaurant, owned by Neven McGuire, has won countless awards for its food, wine and customer service.

Address: Main St, Tuam, Blacklion, Co. Cavan

The Lantern Restaurant , Co. Antrim

The Tartine Restaurant, County Antrim

For a delicious and affordable treat, this is a great spot in Bushmills, providing early bird and vegan options. Also known for its killer cocktails.

Address: 140 Main St, Bushmills, Co. Antrim

Cuffs Bar & Grill, County Antrim

For a jail-house experience, dine at Crumlin Road Gaol in Belfast City. This setting is not only steeped in history, but the food is more than memorable.

Address: 53-55 Crumlin Rd, Belfast, Co. Antrim

The Sooty Olive, County Derry

For great food in the heart of the waterside, the Sooty Olive boasts first-class ingredients and excellent service in a great location. Be sure to put this on your to-eat list when in Derry.

Address: 162 Spencer Rd, Co. Derry

The Phoenix Tavern, County Donegal

For an electric atmosphere and delicious food, this is the perfect stop off for some hearty grub, mouthwatering beers and live music. A local and holidaymakers' favourite when in Bundoran.

Address: Single St, Drumacrin, Bundoran, Co. Donegal

Munster

O'Looneys Bar and Restaurant, County Clare

What is better than enjoying a delicious meal with a fantastic view? This is the perfect place to gaze out to the sea while satisfying your food cravings.

Address: Beech House, Marine Parade, Dough, Lahinch, Co. Clare

Market Lane, County Cork

Featuring great food and drink across two floors, this is the place to go for craft beer, a varied menu, which uses as much locally sourced food as possible, and a warm welcome.

Address: 5-6 Oliver Plunkett St, Centre, Co. Cork

An Corcan, County Kerry

A local restaurant in Waterville, serving mouthwatering dishes. Either eat in, take away, or pop into its yummy bakery for a quick snack.

Address: Centrepoint, Main Street, Waterville, Co. Kerry

An Corcan Restaurant , Co. Tyrone

Pilgrims, County Cork

For farm-to-fork dining to die for, this restaurant is one worth driving cross-country to eat in. Its menu is so diverse, and the produce is all organically grown. Some options available include tomato and fennel haddock stew, pumpkin laksa curry and chocolate-dipped coconut macaroons.

Address: 6 South Square, Townlands, Rosscarbery, Co. Cork

The Bianconi, County Kerry

The Bianconi is home to a head chef who has been providing traditional and fusion dishes for over forty years. Its inn is perfect for a good night's rest, too.

Address: Annadale Rd, Dromavally, Killorglin, Co. Kerry

The Laurels, County Kerry

This pub restaurant has been on the go for almost a century, providing locals and visitors with delicious grub in a vibrant atmosphere.

Address: Main St, Killarney, Co. Kerry

Fisherman's Bar & Skellig Restaurant, County Kerry

If seeking seafood overlooking the water in Portmagee, this is your go-to place.

Address: 2 Harbour View, Portmagee, Co. Kerry

Cornstore Restaurant, County Limerick

If you are in search of quality, fresh and organic ingredients served in an atmospheric space, then this is the place for you.

Address: 19 Thomas St, Co. Limerick

Flanagan's Lane, County Tipperary

Serving top-notch food in Tipperary, it is no wonder why the locals and tourists are such fans of Flanagan's.

Address: Flanagan's Lane, 51 Main St, Co. Tipperary

Connaught

Sangria, County Galway

When in Galway City, head to Sangria for some of the best Sangria, tacos, empanadas and ceviche on the Emerald Isle. Run by a Guatemalan-American husband and wife duo, this place has got some serious character and a fantastic menu that everyone will love.

Address: 19 Middle St, Galway, H91 RX76

Dough Bros, Co. Galway. (facebook.com)

Dough Bros, County Galway

For a pizza perfect experience, you must try their wood-fired pizza and craft beer. This is the place to be!

Address: Cathedral Buildings, 1 Middle St, Co. Galway

Ardagh Restaurant, County Galway

What a treat to dine in a place like this, with such a stunning location, whilst providing the freshest seafood.

Address: Ardagh, Ballyconneely Rd, Clifden, Connemara, Co. Galway

The Helm Restaurant and Bar, County Mayo

Located along the quay of Westport harbour, you'll find The Helm, a great place to treat yourself to some delicious local seafood and an authentic pint of Guinness, either with the family or on a fancy evening out.

Address: The Quay, Cloonmonad, Westport, Co. Mayo

The Tavern Bar, County Mayo

If you like a challenge, you will not be disappointed here because your biggest challenge will be choosing from their extensive food, wine and craft beer menus. You may need a few visits.

Address: Murrisk, Westport, Co. Mayo

Regan's Pub & Restaurant, County Roscommon

This family-run restaurant is a great place for top-class food, a few pints, and a lovely, cosy Irish atmosphere.

Address: The Square, Cloonbrackna, Co. Roscommon

Coach Lane Restaurant, County Sligo

Opt for a dining experience at Coach Lane in the heart of Sligo and you'll quickly see why it's won so many awards over the years. A great choice for everyone!

Address: 2 Lord Edward St, Abbeyquarter North, Co. Sligo

Leinster

Locks Restaurant, County Dublin

One of Dublin's favourite lunch spots, Locks is set canalside and offers some great value for three-course lunch and dinners.

Address: 1 Windsor Terrace, Portobello, Co. Dublin

Beshoff Bros., Co. Dublin

Finnegans Pub, County Dublin

For yummy pub grub in the sun, this is an ideal place for a spot of lunch al fresco as you watch the world go by. Serving delicious food and creamy pints in a welcoming South Dublin atmosphere.

Address: 1 Sorrento Rd, Dalkey, Co. Dublin

Beshoffs, County Dublin

A seaside walk and a Beshoffs supper go hand in hand. Park yourself on a bench facing the sea and indulge in a traditional taste of Ireland.

Address: 12 Harbour Rd, Howth, Co. Dublin

Vintage Kitchen, County Dublin

This popular restaurant specialises in local ingredients located in the heart of Dublin City.

Address: 1 Windsor Terrace, Portobello, Co. Dublin

The Chophouse, Count Dublin

Meat lovers will absolutely love this joint, which serves up the best Irish meat around. But don't worry, vegetarians, there is a menu for you too!

Address: 2 Shelbourne Rd, Co. Dublin

Aroi, County Kilkenny

Only 300 metres from Kilkenny Castle, this is the spot to stop at for some delicious and affordable, authentic Asian street food.

Address: Friary St, Gardens, Co. Kilkenny

Sheehan's Restaurant, County Waterford

Specialising in steak and seafood, this centrally located restaurant is a popular choice for many locals and people visiting Waterford.

Address: 40 Merchants Quay, Co. Waterford

Victoria House, County Waterford

The best spot for music, food and sports in Waterford. Featuring an epic beer garden with superb sea views, an outdoor bar and DJs, this is an ideal choice for a sunny day.

Address: 12 Queen's St, Tramore East, Co. Waterford

The Empire Music Hall, Belfast, Co. Antrim

Uluru, County Waterford

Home to live music, sport and mouth-watering Aussie fare in Waterford.

Address: Dunmore Road, Co. Waterford

Top Pubs

Pubs are one of the cornerstones of Irish culture. On your Irish adventure, you are sure to find a vast amount of pubs all over the country! Here are a few that you absolutely must visit.

Ulster

The Belfast Empire, County Antrim

The Belfast Empire is the heartbeat of the city's live music scene and also hosts a weekly comedy club. It is home to a wide range of entertainment seven nights a week that keeps locals and tourists entertained.

Address: 42 Botanic Ave, Belfast BT7 1JQ, Co. Antrim

Porthole Bar and Restaurant, County Antrim

Everything you could want in a relaxed atmosphere. Featuring an epic backdrop of the Atlantic Ocean, a traditional peat fire, wines from all over the globe and scrumptious local cuisine.

Address: 2 Bayhead Rd, Portballintrae, Co. Antrim

The Atlantic Bar, County Antrim

The best place in town for music heads and known as one of the top spots for live music on the North coast, The Atlantic Bar has a great atmosphere that keeps people coming back time and time again for an entertaining night out.

Address: 43 Main St, Portrush, Co. Antrim

Bushmills Restaurant and Bar, County Antrim

A bar for almost any occasion. Whether you're after an alfresco experience or comfort food in the form of pub grub, this gastropub has it all.

Address: 9 Dunluce Rd, Bushmills, Co. Antrim

Holohan's at the Barge, County Antrim

For a quirky change of scenery, enjoy drinks on this converted barge, with epic views over the Belfast waterfront.

Address: 1 Lanyon Pl, Belfast, Co. Antrim

Tomneys Bar , Co. Tyrone

Walled City Brewing, County Derry

A popular brewpub and restaurant with a great selection of craft beer and international dishes. Beer lovers will be in their element here.

Address: 70 Ebrington St, Co. Derry

Bennigan's Bar, County Derry

This spot is the hub for all things music, with a varied weekly line-up featuring some big names on occasion.

Address: 13 John St, Co. Derry

Wild Atlantic Bar at Grand Central, County Donegal

At the Grand Central Wild Atlantic Bar, there is always something going on. Not to mention that they serve up great drinks and fine value food, all in a vibrant atmosphere.

Address: Main St, Drumacrin, Bundoran, Co. Donegal

Early's Bar, County Donegal

For a real taste of Island nightlife, hop on over to Arranmore Island and head to Early's for a relaxed and fun experience at this traditional Irish island pub.

Address: Leabgarrow, Arranmore Island, Co. Donegal

Tomneys Bar, County Tyrone

In the picturesque village of Moy, you'll find one of the oldest and most traditional Irish pubs on the island: Tomney's Bar. Make sure to stop by for some live music at this award-winning bar.

Address: The Square, Moy, Dungannon, Co. Tyrone

Munster

Kenny's Bar, County Clare

Renowned as one of Clare's landmark pubs, this local sea-side pub is brimming with atmosphere and is a fourth-generation family business.

Address: Main St, Dough, Lahinch, Co. Clare, Ireland

The Bulman Bar, County Cork

Steeped in tradition and located on the outskirts of Kinsale in Summercove, this quaint seaside pub has a log fire to cosy up to while you sip on a refreshing pint or grab a bite to eat.

Address: Summercove, Kinsale, Co. Cork

Armada Bar, County Cork

For dinner like mammy used to make, head to the Armada Bar, where the food is always hearty and home-cooked. With darts, pool and live music, this is the spot for relaxation and entertainment in equal measure.

Address: Market St, Sleveen, Kinsale, Co. Cork

Blue Loo Pub, County Cork

A charming West Cork experience with a lively rooftop beer garden and a casual and relaxed atmosphere, this is a spot to chill on a sunny day or chat with the locals in the evening.

Address: Main street, Monteensudder, Glengarriff, Co. Cork

Turners Bar, County Kerry

A great spot to have the craic and a singalong. Karaoke? Sports? Great value pints? It's all here at Tralee's favourite pub.

Address: 22 Castle St, Tralee, Co. Kerry

The Brogue Inn, Count Kerry

The best spot if you're mad for trad with an award-winning menu and live music in the heart of Tralee (Kerry's capital town), there is no excuse not to stop by The Brogue Inn.

Address: Rock St, Balloonagh, Tralee, Co. Kerry

Dick Mack's Pub and Brewhouse, County Kerry

If it's live music, a variety of craft beer or fine whiskies you are after, then look no further than Dick Mack's when in Dingle. Locals and visitors alike love this place!

Address: 47 Green St, Dingle, Co. Kerry

Dick Mack's Pub and Brewhouse, Co.Kerry

John Benny's Pub, County Kerry

For fantastic food and a great atmosphere you may want to head here for a pint or two, but you must not leave without trying their delicious dishes, especially the seafood!

Address: Strand St, Dingle, Co. Kerry

Killarney Brewing Co., County Kerry

Beer drinking at its finest. Get here hungry and thirsty, so you can appreciate the array of beers on offer. Make sure to try one of their mouth-watering wood-fired pizzas.

Address: Muckross Rd, Killarney, Co. Kerry

The Shire Bar, County Kerry

A *LOTR* fan's dream, this unique *Lord of The Rings* themed bar and cafe is a place you should stop by to get a taste of life in The Shire.

Address: Michael Collins Place, Killarney, Co. Kerry

The Shire Bar, Co. Kerry

South Pole Inn, County Kerry

In the historic home of Tom Crean (the legendary Antarctic explorer), there is a pub where his memory lives on. It prides itself on offering hot food, cold beer and a warm welcome, as well as an array of Tom Crean memorabilia.

Address: Main Street Lower, Gurteen North, Annascaul, Co. Kerry

McCarthy's Pub Restaurant & Undertaker, County Tipperary

This old-school pub in Tipperary promises its customers: "we'll wine you, dine you and bury you". A must-visit, without a doubt!

Address: 17 Main St, Spitalfield, Fethard, Co. Tipperary

The Reg, County Waterford

For an all-round experience, this bar has it all: al fresco dining, late-night hours, five bars, live entertainment, and it is located right in the Viking triangle.

Address: 2 The Mall, Co. Waterford

The Celtic Whiskey Bar, County Kerry

From whiskey to cocktails and craft beers, this spot has the coolest range of bespoke drinks in Kerry.

Address: 93 New St, Killarney, Co. Kerry

The Dingle Pub, County Kerry

Where it is all happening in Dingle! With trad music sessions seven nights a week, dancing, live entertainment and a B&B, The Dingle Pub truly has it all.

Address: Main St, Grove, Dingle, Co. Kerry

Connaught

The Quays Bar and Restaurant, County Galway

This bar and music hall in the heart of Galway is the perfect place to see live music seven nights a week. With a truly unique interior of gothic arches, pews, and stained glass imported from a French medieval church, it truly is a sight in itself.

Address: Quay Ln, Co. Galway

Lowry's Bar, County Galway

There is no excuse not to drop into Connemara's most famous pub when passing through the bustling town of Clifden. Home to live music seven nights a week and Connemara's largest selection of whiskey and gin, you're onto a winner!

Address: Market St, Clifden, Co. Galway

O'Dowd's, County Galway

For a pub that has remained unchanged for decades, this unique bar is intimate and cosy with amazing views over Roundstone Harbour and the Twelve Bens – what a setting for some delicious seafood and a pint!

Address: Main Street, Roundstone, Co. Galway

Cryan's Bar, County Leitrim

This pub boasts amazing live music and mighty craic in the heart of Carrick-on-Shannon.

Address: Bridge Street, Townparks, Carrick-On-Shannon, Co. Leitrim

Ted's Pub, County Mayo

For the best welcome you could ask for, head to Teds! With an all year round roaring open fire, live music and the best craic on the island, you'll not regret your visit.

Address: Cashel South, Achill, Co. Mayo

Lynott's Pub, County Mayo

This teeny-tiny pub is a place where singing is encouraged. Music is its heartbeat, and the setting alone is like something from an old Irish movie.

Address: Cashel, Bunacurry, Co. Mayo

Mickey's Bar at Lavelle's Seaside House, County Mayo

For a scenic setting for a lovely drink, head on over to Mickey's on Achill Island, where you can enjoy a local pint and some hearty pub grub in a beautiful setting.

Address: Dooega, Achill Island, Co. Mayo

Ted's Pub, Achill Island, Co. Mayo

The Beach Bar, County Sligo

This traditional Irish thatched pub is like something from a postcard and will provide the perfect Instagram photo, as well as a delicious pint of the 'black stuff' (aka Guinness). Located across from the ocean, this spot is an absolute must if you fancy a beach bar full of west coast character.

Address: Aughris head, Templeboy, Co. Sligo

The Strand Bar, County Sligo

A welcoming haven run by talented Irish surfers, this local favourite is popular with people of all ages, with love for good music, a great atmosphere and even better: a tempting food menu.

Address: Shore Rd, Carrowbunnaun, Strandhill, Co. Sligo

The Beach Bar, Co. Sligo

Leinster

Johnny Foxes, County Dublin

The highest pub in Ireland and famous for its 'Hooley' Irish dancing and its award-winning seafood restaurant, this pub is a go-to for tourists and locals alike. Cosy up by the fire, or enjoy al fresco dining as you gaze out over the Dublin mountains.

Address: Glencullen, Co. Dublin

The Brazen Head, County Dublin

One of Ireland's oldest pubs, it cannot be overlooked when in Dublin City for a night out. Founded in 1198, this historic establishment is definitely worth a visit or two.

Address: 20 Lower Bridge St, Usher's Quay, Co. Dublin

The Porterhouse, County Dublin

A craft beer haven with a central location, great pub food and a dreamy craft beer menu, this is a perfect choice when in Temple Bar.

Address: 47 Nassau St, Co. Dublin

The Temple Bar Pub, County Dublin

Dublin's most iconic pub, this pub is hard to miss when strolling the streets of Temple Bar. It has the only licensed beer garden in the area, so it's perfect for a sunny afternoon pint.

Address: 47-48, Temple Bar, Co. Dublin

The Left Bank, County Kilkenny

A pub with a host of bar areas to choose from, this former banking hall is famous in Kilkenny for its live entertainment, its unique

Victorian style and its many spaces to enjoy an epic night out.

Address: 1 The Parade, Gardens, Co. Kilkenny

James Griffin Pub, County Meath

For a true Irish welcome and a great pint, *Trim Heritage Town* has more to offer than an epic castle, just head to James Griffin for a traditional Irish experience.

Address: 21 High St, Trim, Co. Meath

Jack Meades, County Waterford

Whether you want to enjoy the Beer Garden, Loft Bar, Traditional Bar or Gastro Bar, the choice is yours at Jack Meades, a pub that is different from most you'll find.

Address: Cheekpoint, Co. Waterford

Phil Grimes Pub, County Waterford

With an extensive list of bespoke beers, wines and spirits in a cool atmosphere, it's no wonder that locals' consider Phil Grimes their favourite pub in Waterford.

Address: 60 Johnstown, Co. Waterford

Sean's Bar, County Westmeath

Conveniently located in Athlone, halfway between Dublin and Galway, Ireland's oldest bar (founded around 900 AD) awaits your visit. Sean's Bar has won many awards and for a good reason: it has been one of the best pubs for drinks, chats and music for over a thousand years!

Address: 13 Main St, Athlone, Co. Westmeath

The Enniskerry Inn, County Wicklow

With live music every weekend, great pub food and a B&B (so you don't have to go far), this is the perfect spot to stop by when passing through the charming village of Enniskerry.

Address: Church Hill, Enniskerry, Co. Wicklow

Top Cafes

Ulster

Panky Doos, County Antrim

A haven for waffles and pancakes, this family-run cafe is the cutest spot to enjoy breakfast.

Address: Eglinton St, Portrush, Co. Antrim

Sean's Bar, Co. Westmeath

The Dock, County Antrim

Want some coffee in the Titanic Quarter? Founded to bring life to the concrete Titanic Quarter, The Dock (which has an inspirational backstory) has become a local favourite.

Address: 2K Queens Rd, Belfast, Co. Antrim

Kraken Fish and Chips, County Antrim

For the freshest and most authentic fish and chips around, head to Kraken for lunch or supper.

Address: 25 Lansdowne Cres, Portrush, Co. Antrim

The Hard Boiled Egg Cafe, County Cavan

Whether it's a traditional Irish breakfast, a scrumptious lunch, or a tasty milkshake, this is the best cafe in the area.

Address: Dublin Rd, Tullymongan Upper, Co. Cavan

Pyke 'n' Pommes, County Derry

For anyone looking an authentic street food experience, this internationally-acclaimed and award-winning street food spot is a revolution in Derry.

Address: Strand Rd, Co. Derry

The Coffee Tree, County Derry

Great value, delectable snacks, and a central location all make this a go-to spot for locals and visitors to Derry.

Address: 49 Strand Rd, Co. Derry

Buoys and Gulls, County Donegal

A cafe in the bustling seaside town of Bundoran which aims to bring its customers the best Irish products, carefully sourced from around the country.

Address: Ocean View, W End, Magheracar, Bundoran, Co. Donegal

The Jolly Sandwich Bar, County Fermanagh

For a delicious homemade breakfast, lunch or brunch, this hidden gem in Ulster is a must!

Address: 3 Darling St, Enniskillen, Co. Fermanagh

Munster

Three Fools Coffee, County Cork

There's nothing foolish about this spot; a haven for coffee lovers, meet-ups and people-watching when in Cork City.

Address: Grand Parade, Centre, Co. Cork

The Bakehouse , Co. Tipperary

Milk Market Cafe, County Cork

Stop by this colourful and quirky cafe in the centre of Kinsale, and make sure to try their milkshakes.

Address: 3 Market St, Sleveen, Kinsale, Co. Cork

Cafe Du Parc, County Kerry

This cafe serves not only mouthwatering breakfasts but also lunch, brunch, dinner and cocktails. Visit here at any time of the day, and you're sure to have a fantastic feed.

Address: Killarney Plaza Hotel & Spa, Kenmare Placa, Killarney, Co. Kerry

7th Heaven Bistro and Cafe, County Kerry

Whether you are after a traditional Irish breakfast, a quick lunch or a main course, 7th Heaven Bistro and Cafe is a great spot in the centre of Tralee.

Address: 41 Ashe St, Tralee, Co. Kerry

Valentia Ice Cream Parlour and Farmhouse Dairy, County Kerry

If you are an ice cream lover, then do not miss the opportunity to try some of the freshest ice creams you will ever encounter. Here you will not only have delicious dairy treats, but the cherry on top is the view.

Address: Kilbeg East, Valentia Island, Co. Kerry

Coffee Pot Cafe, County Kerry

This homey cafe is located in the Gap of Dunloe, and with a warm Irish welcome, it won't just be the scenery that leaves an imprint on you.

Address: Gap of Dunloe, Beaufort, Co. Kerry

Rift Coffee, County Limerick

If you are a coffee connoisseur, you will want to try out the different and ever-changing coffees on offer at this busy coffee shop in County Limerick.

Address: 30 Upper Mallow St, Co. Limerick

The Bakehouse, County Tipperary

In the heart of Cashel you'll find The Bakehouse, a local favourite for a traditional breakfast, lunch, lovely cakes and fresh coffee, as well as being a great place to relax and watch the world go by.

Address: 6 Main St, St. Dominick's Abbey, Cashel, Co. Tipperary

Cafe Du Parc, Co. Kerry

Connaught

Goya's Cafe, County Galway

In the heart of Galway, you'll find Goya's Cafe and Bakery: ideal for breakfast, lunch or a sweet treat.

Address: 2-3 Kirwan's Ln, Co. Galway

Coco Cafe, County Galway

A cafe with tasty treats, great coffee, and an amazing backdrop of Galway Bay, The Burren and Cliffs of Moher.

Address: Salthill Rd Upper, Co. Galway

Upstairs Downstairs Cafe, County Galway

Award-winning Irish speciality coffee, tea, and freshly baked pastries – what more could you ask for?

Address: Main St, Clifden, Co. Galway

This Must Be The Place, County Mayo

With an array of tasty meals and treats, this place in Westport lives up to its name, without a doubt!

Address: High St, Cahernamart, Westport, Co. Mayo

Shells Cafe, County Sligo

Great coffee, great views and awesome food, this is the best little seaside cafe to enjoy when in Strandhill. It even offers some kick-ass vegan and vegetarian treats.

Address: Seafront, Strandhill, Co. Sligo

Mammy Johnston's Ice Cream Parlour, County Sligo

Your taste buds will thank you for stopping off here. There is delicious homemade ice cream, crepes and coffee on offer at Mammy Johnston's.

Address: Shore Rd, Carrowbunnaun, Strandhill, Co. Sligo

Leinster

Queen of Tarts, County Dublin

Serving the best breakfasts and brunch in Dublin, this cafe is run by two sisters who trained as pastry chefs in New York.

Address: Cow's Ln, Dame St, Temple Bar, Co. Dublin

Clement & Pekoe, County Dublin

For speciality coffee in Dublin, this is considered to be one of the best brews in all of City. Try for yourself!

Address: 50 William St S, Dublin 2, Co. Dublin

Queen of Tarts , Co. Dublin

Offbeat Donuts, County Dublin

To satisfy the cravings, Offbeat is a revolution in Ireland when it comes to unique and delicious donuts – they are perfect for a quick sweet snack or road trip treat.

Address: Jervis Shopping Centre, 125 Abbey Street Upper, Co. Dublin

Pennefeather Cafe, County Kilkenny

A favourite of both locals and tourists. For home-style cooking and hearty lunches in Kilkenny City, head over to Pennefeather Cafe.

Address: 10 High St, Gardens, Co. Kilkenny

Powerscourt, Co. Wicklow (commons.wikimedia.org)

Maguires Cafe and Gift Shop, County Meath

Have a browse in the gift shop here before chowing down on some delicious grub, homemade scones or tasty cakes. This place is very popular with local families and visitors exploring the heritage area.

Address: Hill of Tara, Co. Meath

Harvest Home Bakery, County Meath

Think breads, pastries, cakes, homemade honey and jams as well as specially made customised treats, and you've got it all at Harvest Home Bakery.

Address: 18 Market St, Townparks South, Trim, Co. Meath

Tra Coffee Roasters, County Waterford

Bringing you the best coffee beans around, sourced sustainably and tasting absolutely divine. Coffee lovers will be in their element here.

Address: Unit 4, Riverstown Business Park, Tramore, Co. Waterford

The Happy Pear, County Wicklow

With a mission to create a healthier, happier world while serving some of the freshest, vegan and vegetarian meals you'll find, The Happy Pear really have created an inspiring empire.

Address: Church Rd, Rathdown Lower, Greystones, Co. Wicklow

Powerscourt Avoca Cafe, County Wicklow

This is the perfect place to stop for some great food and a coffee while exploring Powerscourt Estate.

Address: Powerscourt House, Enniskerry, Co. Wicklow

Top Live Music Venues

Ulster

Peadar O'Donnell's & Gweedore Bar, County Derry

Situated next to each other, O'Donnell's is famous for its traditional music, while The Gweedore Bar is a live bands venue with contemporary music.

Address: 63 Waterloo St, Co. Derry

Tig Choili Pub , Co. Galway

Grand Central, County Donegal

With a dedicated live music calendar, this venue located at The Grand Central Hotel in Bundoran offers up impressive performances around the clock.

Address: Main St, Drumacrin, Bundoran, Co. Donegal

Munster

The Corner House, County Cork

Cork's house of music! This is the best spot in Cork for traditional Irish music, a creamy pint and a cosy atmosphere.

Address: 7 Coburg St, Victorian Quarter, Co. Cork

Killarney Grand, County Kerry

A killer spot for a great night out that appeals to people of all ages, The Killarney Grand has in-house entertainment seven nights a week in the heart of Killarney.

Address: Main St, Killarney, Co. Kerry

Connaught

Tig Choili, County Galway

This is the home of traditional Irish music in Galway and should not be missed when in the city. Tigh Choili also has fresh-baked pizzas and unique, custom-brewed beers.

Address: Mainguard St, The Latin Quarter, Co. Galway

Matt Molloy's, County Mayo

Voted the 'best live venue' in Connaught in 2014 and 2015, they must be doing something right. Matt Molloy's attracts a steady string of locals and tourists who come back, time and time again.

Address: Bridge St, Cahernamart, Westport, Co. Mayo

Leinster

Whelan's, County Dublin

Dublin's most-loved live music venue. Founded in 1989, Whelan's continues to be the most thriving music venue in the capital.

Address: 25 Wexford St, Portobello, Co. Dublin

Matt the Millers, County Kilkenny

Voted Ireland's 'best music pub of the year' in 2017, Matt the Millers has five on-site bars, providing you with live music and DJs.

Address: 1 John Street Lower, College Park, Co. Kilkenny

Itineraries

3 Day Itinerary: The Quick Eastern Getaway

Dublin to Wicklow

Day 1

Morning

- Pick up your car and get ready for some sightseeing in and around Dublin. The choices are endless when it comes to things to see in this bustling city.

- Explore the famous area of Temple Bar, where you can admire the colourful streets, cobbled stone walkways and enjoy some breakfast/coffee at Queen of Tarts.

- From here you can visit Trinity College, home to the Book of Kells and one of the most impressive libraries around.

Afternoon

- Pick up your car and get ready for some sightseeing in and around Dublin. The choices are endless when it comes to things to see in this bustling city.

- Stop off for some pub grub at The Brazen Head.

- Then take a tour in Kilmainham Gaol (jail) a place steeped in history and where many prominent figures were held prisoner during the 1916 rising. Booking this in advance is strongly recommended.

Evening

- Enjoy dinner, drinks and live music in The Porterhouse and be sure to try some of their local brews while you're there.

Temple Bar, Co. Dublin (pixabay.com / Skitterphoto)

Accommodation

- **Splashing Out**: The Shelbourne Hotel, The Radisson Blu Hotel

- **Mid Range**: The Merrion Hotel

- **Affordable**: Fitzsimons Hotel

Insider Tip: Traffic in Dublin can be very busy at peak times, just like any other city. It is also worth noting that many of the streets in the city operate one-way systems, so be cautious when driving and follow the signs and directions on your GPS system to avoid any problems. Almost everywhere in Dublin is paid parking, so don't forget to place a valid parking ticket in the windscreen and make sure the parking space is permitted, as some can be reserved or private. Parking meters can be found on almost every main street, some may be hidden so be sure to take a walk along the road to find the metre for a ticket. If in doubt don't hesitate to ask a local, who are always willing to help.

Day 2

Morning

- After enjoying a hotel breakfast, head towards Powerscourt House and Gardens in County Wicklow. This is a one-hour drive from Dublin City. This area will take at least 60 minutes to explore, and is home to enchanting woodlands, manicured lawns and a towering waterfall.

- Grab a bite to eat at Powerscourt's Avoca Café at Powerscourt, or wait until later for a lunch dish at the original Avoca.

Afternoon

- Drive south to Glendalough to explore the stunning Wicklow Mountains and take on a short hike on one of the many trails.

- Continue onwards to the town of Avoca, Wicklow. Avoca Traditional Handweavers is Ireland's oldest woollen mill dating back to 1723.

- Enjoy a lunch of delicious homemade food and artisan produce at its cafe.

Evening

- Enjoy a restful evening in the 'Garden of Ireland' – a colloquial term for County Wicklow.

Glendalough, Co. Wicklow (flickr.com)

Day 3

Morning

- Return to Dublin via the quaint coastal towns of Greystones located in County Wicklow and Dalkey in South County Dublin.

- Grab breakfast in the famous vegetarian/vegan cafe, The Happy Pear, on the main street in Greystones. Prepare to wait in a line as the place is very popular, for good reason.

- Then, take a stroll through the historic town of Dalkey to see Dalkey Castle.

- Continue down to the coast, known as the Dublin Riviera where you can admire some absolutely stunning mansions on Dublin's most expensive road en route back to the capital city.

Guinness Store House, Co. Dublin (commons.wikimedia.org)

Afternoon

- Take a tour of the Guinness Storehouse and learn the steps to pouring a perfect pint of the black stuff.

Evening

- Head back into the city centre and enjoy some dinner and drinks at The Vintage Kitchen which is BYOB, and continue on to Whelans for some brilliant live music.

3 Day Itinerary: From Rat Race to Rural

Dublin to Portlaoise via the Wicklow Mountains

Day 1

Morning

- Pick up your car and begin a day of exploring Dublin City, starting with the bustling district of Temple Bar as well as the famous Trinity College and the nature haven of St Stephens Green for a late morning stroll. Enjoy breakfast at Brother Hubbard to set you up for the afternoon ahead.

Afternoon

- Take a tour of the historic Kilmainham Gaol which will give you a great insight into Ireland's history and while in the area, stop off at Rascals Brewing Company for a stonebaked pizza and a flight of their famous local beer.

Evening

- Have some pub grub in Temple Bar and continue on to Whelans for some live music.

Day 2

Morning

- Drive one hour to Roundwood in County Wicklow, one of Ireland's highest towns located at 238 metres above sea level, to enjoy fresh air, beautiful landscapes and lush walks. Grab a coffee and bite to eat at Sugar Mountain Cafe and Bistro.

Afternoon

- From here, continue on the country Wicklow roads towards Glendalough to get deep into the heart of the Wicklow Mountains. Here you can explore the area by foot, opting for one of the many hiking trails available including The Spinc, one of the most popular trails. You will come across the medieval monastic settlement here, dating back to the 6th-century which is a popular spot to explore mid hike.

Evening

- From Glendalough, drive 90 minutes to the town of Portlaoise, Count Laois. Check into your hotel and spend the evening having dinner and drinks at Jeremiah Grant Bar and Eatery.

Day 3

Morning

- Spend the morning exploring Portlaoise, including The Rock of Dunamase a popular historic attraction overlooking the valley.

Afternoon

- Stop off at Treacy's pub, one of Ireland's oldest traditional pubs dating back 200 years, offering mouthwatering Irish pub grub and a smashing Guinness.

The Donaghmore Famine Workhouse Museum is a must see after lunch to gauge the stories of the families who lived and died behind these walls during one of the most difficult times in Irish history.

Evening

- En route back to Dublin you have the option to stop off at Kildare Village Outlet - a popular place that locals love to go to shop brand names at discount prices. It's a great way to bring back souvenirs or treat yourself on a budget.

- Spend the evening in the small town of Ranelagh, an upper class suburb of South Dublin, where you can have dinner and drinks at Taphouse.

Wicklow Mountain Drive (tourismireland.com)

3 Day Itinerary: Majestic Ring of Kerry

Day 1

Morning

- Pick up your car in Cork and drive just 90 minutes to the town of Killarney in the heart of Kerry. This is a great base to explore the surrounding areas of Killarney National Park as well as the town itself with its many traditional pubs, live music and historical sights. Stop for some coffee and breakfast in Cafe Du Parc when you arrive to set you up for the day.

Afternoon

- Just a half hour drive from the city, you will find some great places to enjoy including Muckross House (take the guided tour here, it's worth every cent), Ross Castle and the impressive Torc Waterfall. You can easily spend the entire afternoon losing yourself in the nature of the national park.

Evening

- Head back to Killarney and if you are a fan of craft beer and pizza, do not miss out on Killarney Brewing Company, which has a great selection of beer, brewed in house and woodfired pizza which is the perfect combination after a day of adventure. After dinner, spend the rest of the evening listening to live traditional music at Killarney Grand, which is offered seven nights a week.

Day 2

Morning

- After breakfast either at the hotel or in town, make your way towards Killorglin, a popular town, famous for being only 15 minutes away from Ireland's highest mountain Mt Carrauntoohil.

- It is also only 40 minutes away from Mt Brandon, Ireland's second highest mountain, so the opportunities for hiking and mountain climbing are endless, when in Killorglin.

Ross Castle, Co. Kerry (commons.wikimedia.org)

Afternoon

- From here, you can continue to Portmagee, where you can opt for a boat trip to the famous Skellig Islands, which featured in *Star Wars*, and is well known for its steep mountainside steps that lead to the impressive 6th-century monastery at the top.

- From here, you can also cross the bridge to Valentia Island and climb to the top of the Valentia lighthouse for some stunning views before continuing on to the town of Waterville if you fancy seeing where Charlie Chaplin spent many a summer in the 60s.

Evening

- Grab some delicious dinner in the heart of Waterville at An Corcan Restaurant.

Killorglin, Co. Kerry (commons.wikimedia.org)

Day 3

Morning

- Set off from Waterville towards Sneem and Kenmare, but make sure to stop off at Caherdaniel beach, a stunning spot to relax and admire the scenery. The town itself is home to some tiny artisan stores which line the village laneways, as well as Derrynane House, late home to the revolutionary leader Daniel O' Connell.

Afternoon

- Stop by the charming village of Sneem, before heading to the bigger town of Kenmare, where you should most definitely have a seafood lunch at Tom Crean's restaurant, Ireland's famous Antarctic explorer.

Evening

- From here, continue on back to Cork where you can spend the evening having dinner at The Raven Bar followed by some more drinks accompanied by music at The Corner House.

5 Day Itinerary: The West Island Discovery

Shannon, Inismore, Galway, Mayo, Achill island

Day 1

Morning

- Pick up your car at Shannon airport and head one hour towards Galway City, where you will explore the city of tribes, recommended on foot. Have some breakfast at The Little Lane Coffee Company, in between wandering the cobbled streets and browsing the unique shops.

Afternoon

- Walk to Salthill and take in the atmosphere of the promenade, visit the Spanish Arch and try Galway Bay oysters for lunch at John Keoghs Gastro pub back in the city.

- Make sure to listen to the buskers liven up Quay St, Shop St and High St.

Evening

- Head to Tig Coili Pub tonight to listen to some Irish music in the most famous bar in the city, where many of Ireland's best musicians have played.

Spanish Arch. Co. Galway (commons.wikimedia.org)

Day 2

Morning/Afternoon

- From Galway, head towards Rossaveel only 45 minutes west, where you'll take the ferry to your first island, Inis Mor, the largest of the Aran islands. Take the morning passenger ferry and come back the next day.

- Make sure to visit the cliffside fort of Dun Aonghasa, described as the most magnificent barbaric monument in Europe.

- Inis Mor is a great place to learn about Irish culture and tradition, as well as observing the locals speaking Irish to each other. Opt to hire a bike and see the island from a different perspective.

Evening

- Spend the evening at Joe Wattys pub where you can have traditional Irish food and drinks with live music, in a real old school Irish pub, island style.

Day 3

Morning

- Having arrived back to Rossaveal, pick up your car at the parking area and continue the road trip towards the seaside towns of Roundstone and Clifden and on to Westport, County Mayo.

- Roundstone is famous for its annual regatta each July but also for its pristine beaches of Dog's Bay beach and Gurteen Beach, as well as its cafes, craft-shops and pubs.

- Clifden, often referred to as the capital of the Connemara region, is well-known by tourists and a popular stop over on Irish road trips.

- Have coffee and a tasty treat at Walsh's Bakery and Coffee Shop.

Afternoon/Evening

- Continue on for one hour and 15 minutes to reach Westport, County Mayo - a bustling, vibrant and colourful town just minutes from the coast.

- Make sure to visit Cupan Tae for some delicious afternoon tea right in the heart of town.

- Visit Westport House, home of Grace O' Malley, Ireland's pirate queen, as well as Westport Harbour, lined with bars and restaurants set opposite a stunning coastal view.

- If you feel up for another hike, try one of the most famous pilgrimages in Ireland, Croagh Patrick, which will reward you with fantastic views of Clew Bay and all the islands.

Day 4

Morning/Afternoon

- After breakfast, take the one hour leisurely drive out to the largest of Ireland's islands, Achill Island, which is connected by bridge. Here you can either opt to drive the island or park up at the hotel and rent bikes to explore the coast. The roads here are even narrower than normal as well as being windy and some steep, so take caution driving and cycling here.

Evening

- Have some dinner and drinks at Amethyst Bar this evening and if you want a real traditional experience, be sure to check out Lynott's Pub, a tiny old thatched Irish pub, for a couple of pints.

Day 5

Morning

- On your last day, it's time to leave the island and take the journey back to Shannon, but stop at Gieltys for a bite to eat before you set off.

Afternoon

- Don't miss out on The Museum Of Irish Country Life, which is free, and an absolute must do, to get a good idea of the way of Irish life through the ages. Be sure to take your time here and enjoy the exhibitions.

Evening

- Head to the Old Lodge Gastropub for some grub if you have time, which isn't far from Shannon Airport.

Inis Mor, Co. Galway (commons.wikimedia.org)

Day 1

Morning/Afternoon

- Pick up your car and take your time exploring the city of Belfast including, the famous Titanic Quarter, Peace Wall, St George's Market and Crumlin Road Gaol.

- Be sure to have a morning coffee and some breakfast at Maggie Mays Botanic Café.

- Later on, when you are feeling peckish again, go to Sawers, Belfast's much loved deli for some fresh lunch options to either takeaway or eat in.

Evening

- Spend the evening lapping up the panoramic view over the city at Babel Rooftop Bar and Kitchen, serving food and drinks in a chic atmosphere, as well as live music.

Day 2

Morning

- Grab some breakfast and coffee at The Coffee House Bistro to set you up for the morning before taking the journey to the north coast towards the Glens of Antrim, stopping off along the way for photo opportunities.

Afternoon

- Continue on to Ballycastle on the north-eastern most coastal point of Ireland, where you can take a walk around town visiting the marina, The Ballycastle Museum and having a fish and chips lunch at Mortons.

Evening

- Enjoy dinner and drinks at House of McDonnell, the pub that time forgot. If you are a wine connoisseur, you can enjoy some delicious wine and a great atmosphere at the Central Wine Bar after dinner.

Croagh Patrick, Co. Mayo (commons.wikimedia.org)

Day 3

Morning/Afternoon

- Take the ferry to Rathlin Island where you can spend the day.

- Visit the Boathouse Visitor Centre to learn about the shipwrecks off the island's shores.

Evening

- Return to Ballycastle for the night, spending the evening having dinner at Thirty Nine Steak and Seafood Restaurant.

Day 4

Morning

- Drive towards Bushmills, stopping at the very impressive Giant's Causeway and Carrick-a-Rede Rope Bridge, which will set your heart racing as you walk across it.

Afternoon

- Upon arrival in Bushmills, take a whiskey tour at the famous Bushmills Distillery, which certainly cannot be missed.

Evening

- Make your way to Bushmills Restaurant and Bar for some locally sourced food in a truly cosy atmosphere.

Day 5

Morning

- Take a visit to the Giant's Causeway & Bushmills Heritage Railway museum this morning.

Afternoon/Evening

- Take the one hour journey back to Belfast and spend the evening at White's, Belfast's oldest tavern, for some food and drinks this evening.

5 Day Itinerary: The Heritage Haven

Dublin, Meath, Louth

Day 1

Morning

- Pick up your car and spend the day exploring all that Dublin has to offer. Begin the morning with a coffee or some breakfast at Bittersweet Cafe before taking in sights including, Trinity College and its impressive library and Temple Bar.

Titanic Centre, Belfast, Co. Antrim (commons.wikimedia.org)

Afternoon

- Spend the afternoon at The Guinness Storehouse, where you will learn the unique brewing process of the most famous drink in Ireland, as well as getting the chance to pour your own. Take in the panoramic view of Dublin City from The Gravity Bar at the top of the building once the tour ends.

Evening

- Spend the evening at The Vintage Cocktail Club trying some of the tastiest cocktails in one of the trendiest places in Dublin.

Day 2

All Day

- Take the one hour drive from Dublin to Trim, home of Trim Castle, which was used for the filming of *Braveheart*. The heritage town is great to stroll around and the castle is a must see. Grab a 99 ice cream in the local sweet shop and spend some time exploring the castle grounds, just as the locals do.

Day 3

Morning

- Today you will have a short drive to The Hill of Tara, an ancient ceremonial and burial site, where you can see passage tombs and burial mounds from the Neolithic age to the Iron age.

- Make sure to stop at the cafe and gift shop for a browse, and to try their delicious scones and traditional Irish grub. The gift shop has some one of a kind souvenir ideas as well as many great books based on Ireland.

Afternoon

- Continue to Newgrange to explore this exceptionally large grand passage tomb, dating back to 3200 BC, making it older than Stonehenge and the Egyptian Pyramids.

- Continue on to the town of Drogheda, where you will stay this evening.

Evening

- This evening have dinner and drinks at Goodwins Steakhouse Grill and Bar.

Newrange, Co. Meath (tourismireland.ie)

Day 4

Morning

- Today, take your time exploring the town of Drogheda, making sure to visit St Peter's Church, where you can see Oliver Plunkett's head and bones as well as Melifont Abbey and Beaulieu House and Garden.

Afternoon

- Take an afternoon drive to the beaches close to Drogheda including, Laytown, Bettystown or Termonfeckin, and have a fish and chips lunch by the beach.

Milmount, Drogheda, Co. Louth (commons.wikimedia.org)

Evening

- Head to the Hops Bar for some dinner and drinks in a local Irish pub setting.
- Stay tonight in Drogheda.

Day 5

Morning/Afternoon

- On your last day, you can drive the coast towards Dublin making a detour to the popular seaside towns of Lusk and Skerries if time allows.
- Spend the afternoon ticking off the sights you missed out on in Dublin, or perhaps want to revisit.

Evening

- Spend the evening having dinner and beer tasting at the Porterhouse brew pub in the heart of the city.

7 Day Itinerary: The Whopper Week

Dublin, Kilkenny, Kerry, Galway

Day 1

Morning

- Pick up your car and spend the day exploring all that Dublin has to offer. Begin the morning with a coffee or some breakfast at Bittersweet Cafe before taking in sights including, Trinity College and its impressive library and Temple Bar.
- Grab some morning coffee at Queen of Tarts in Temple Bar.

Afternoon

- Don't miss the opportunity to pop into Offbeat donuts for some delicious one of a kind doughnuts, a local favourite.

Evening

- Enjoy the buzz of Temple Bar this evening, including a visit to the Temple Bar Pub, which will be very lively on the weekend, along with the rest of the surrounding bars.

- Stay the night in Dublin at your preferred accommodation as listed previously.

Grafton Street, Co. Dublin (commons.wikimedia.org)

Day 2

Morning

- Drive one hour and 45 minutes to Kilkenny, where you can spend the morning exploring Kilkenny Castle, St Canices Cathedral and the many medieval lanes of the city.

Afternoon

- Head out of the city towards Thomastown, a small town full of traditional pubs and quirky streets as well as being home to the impressive Mt Juliet Estate, an ideal place to stroll around and take beautiful photos.

Evening

- Have dinner and drinks at Matt the Millers Bar and Restaurant, known as Ireland's best music pub.

Day 3

Morning

- Drive to Killarney, stopping off at The Rock of Cashel on your way, which is one of Ireland's most spectacular sites.

Afternoon

- Continue on towards Killarney and spend the afternoon exploring the bustling town and for *Lord of The Rings* fans, be sure to pop into The Shire Bar and Cafe for some drinks and perhaps a bite to eat.

Evening

- Settle down for the evening listening to live music and eating traditional Irish food at The Laurels, a traditional Killarney pub, run by the same family for over a century.

Day 4

Morning

- Today, set off on your journey through Killarney National Park, visiting Muckross House, Torc Waterfall and Ross Castle, but first, set yourself up for the day with breakfast at The Coffee Pot Cafe.

Afternoon

- If you fancy taking on some of the famous narrow and windy roads of Kerry, head towards The Gap of Dunloe or Molls Gap for a glimpse at a picture-perfect setting, making you feel like you're on a movie set.

Evening

- Return to Killarney town for another night. Spend the evening at The Celtic Whiskey Bar and Larder, voted one of the 'Flavours of the Wild Atlantic Way' by Discover Ireland.

Day 5

Morning/Afternoon

- Today will be a long morning drive, just over two and a half hours, taking you towards Galway where you will stay two nights.

- Enjoy the drive and stop off along the way at Adare Manor and Bunratty Castle.

Evening

- Upon arrival in Galway, check in to your hotel and go out to have an awesome pizza at the famous Dough Bros, followed by drinks and live music at the ever popular Tig Coili traditional Irish pub.

Day 6

Morning

- Today, you can head into the city for a spot of breakfast at Goya's cafe tucked away on the charming Kirwan's Lane before taking a coastal drive to the towns of Roundstone and Clifden, which are very popular amongst tourists and locals.

Afternoon

- Spend the afternoon taking in the atmosphere of the coastal towns and scenery along the way.

- Stop at O' Dowds of Roundstone for a bite to eat this afternoon.

Kilkenny Castle, Co. Kilkenny (commons.wikimedia.org)

Evening

- Tonight, why not try the famous Galway Bay oysters with a pint of Guinness at one of the many traditional pubs in the city, followed by some live music?

- Stay tonight in Galway City.

Day 7

Morning

- Today is your last day and you will get the chance to spend the morning exploring Galway City, including the Spanish Arch, St Nicholas Church and of course a stroll down the many medieval streets in the Latin Quarter, where you can browse one of a kind stores and coffee shops.

Salthill, Co. Galway (commons.wikimedia.org)

Afternoon

- If you feel up for it, take a thirty minute walk to Salthill Promenade which was the setting for the famous song, 'Galway Girl', before the drive back to Dublin.

- Stop for a spot of brunch at Coco Cafe Salthill.

Evening

- Head to the oldest pub in Dublin, The Brazen Head, for some drinks and delicious food. The pub dates back to 1198, so there is plenty of history there.

7 Day Itinerary: Ireland's Sunny South-Eastern Discovery

Dublin to Waterford

Day 1

Morning

- Pick up your car in Dublin and spend the day exploring the sights of the city.

- Make your way around the iconic Temple Bar, Stephens Green and Trinity College.

Afternoon

- This afternoon, choose between your choice of a Jameson Distillery tour or Guinness Storehouse tour, or both if you have the time.

Evening

- Head to Whelans this evening for some great live music, a true local's favourite, after having a delicious dinner at The Chophouse gastro pub in Ballsbridge, just south of the city centre.

- Stay the night in Dublin at your choice of accommodation.

Day 2

Morning

- Today, you will drive towards Powerscourt House and Gardens in County Wicklow, about an hour's drive from Dublin City.

- Stretching over 47 acres, this beautiful area can take up the whole day to explore, including the 121 metre waterfall.

Stephen's Green, Co. Dublin (commons.wikimedia.org)

Afternoon

- From here, you can take the short drive to the Sugarloaf Mountain for a short but steep hike, with amazing views over Dublin Bay and The Wicklow Mountains.

Evening

- Head to The Enniskerry Inn, located in the charming town that Disney chose to film 'Disenchanted' in 2021 for some dinner and drinks this evening.

Day 3

Morning

- From here, drive south to Glendalough to explore the stunning Wicklow Mountains and take on a short hike on one of the many trails. We recommend The Spinc which is the most popular and most accessible for anyone with a good level of fitness.

Afternoon

- Continue onwards to Avoca traditional handweavers to browse Ireland's oldest woollen mill dating back to 1723 and to try some delicious homemade food at the food halls and cafe.

- After Avoca, make your way towards Waterford City, stopping off in the town of Gorey for a wander, before continuing to Waterford City, which is the oldest city in Ireland and is steeped in history.

- Spend the rest of the afternoon visiting the Waterford Crystal Visitor Centre, the stone fortress of Reginald's Tower, Bishops Palace and The Medieval Museum.

- Try some steak or seafood at the popular Sheehan's restaurant and then continue on to Phil Grimes pub for some pints and live music upstairs.

- Stay tonight in Waterford.

Day 4

Morning

- From Waterford, make your way towards Tramore, one of Ireland's most popular holiday destinations. Here, you can opt to try surfing and other watersports.

Afternoon/Evening

- Make sure to visit the beautiful Japanese Gardens, see the Waterford Racecourse or check out the Tramore Amusement Park for a bit of adventure for the kids or kids at heart.

Day 5

Morning

- Today, you will go north back towards Wexford, but take a detour to Fethard on Sea, located on the Hook Peninsula, known as Ireland's 'sunniest' corner.

- This small village will take you back in time with its traditional pubs and fishing village vibe. Be sure to try some of the best seafood here, which is caught fresh in the local waters.

Afternoon/Evening

- Spend the afternoon visiting Hook Lighthouse, the haunted Loftus Hall, Duncannon Fort and of course the beautiful beaches.

Day 6

Morning

- From Fethard on Sea, take the short drive towards Curracloe Beach, one of Ireland's best beaches and the spot Steven Spielberg chose for his opening scene in the movie *Saving Private Ryan*. This beach was also featured in the Saoirse Ronan movie *Brooklyn*.

Afternoon

- Continue north towards Dublin, stopping off in the quaint seaside village of Greystones, County Wicklow, where you can eat some lunch at the Happy Pear.

- Park the car and venture off on the Greystones to Bray cliff walk, which will provide beautiful coastal views.

Glendalough Mountains, Co. Wicklow (commons.wikimedia.org)

Day 7

Morning

- Today, you will drive back to Dublin but make sure to stop off in Dalkey where you can explore the mansions in Dublin's 'riviera' and marvel at the views from Dalkey Hill over Dublin City, The Wicklow Mountains and Dublin Bay.

Afternoon

- Have some lunch at one of the town's award winning restaurants, before visiting the Dalkey Heritage Centre set in a 14th-century Norman castle.

Evening

- Continue back to Dublin and spend the evening at the Bord Gais theatre enjoying a show.

10 Day Itinerary: The Wild Atlantic Tenner

West Cork to Donegal

Day 1

Morning

- Pick up your car and spend the morning exploring Cork City including St Anne's Church, The English Market, stopping at Liberty Grill for a delicious brunch.

Afternoon

- This afternoon, take the ten kilometre trip to visit Blarney Castle, famous for the Blarney Stone which is set to give anyone who kisses it the gift of the gab.

- Continue driving towards the fabulous area of West Cork where you will stay tonight in Kinsale.

Evening

- Head to the Silent Banjo, a local hangout and one of the best pubs in Kinsale.

Hook Lighthouse, Co. Wexford (commons.wikimedia.org)

Day 2

Morning

- This morning, have a stroll around the pretty village of Kinsale, stopping at Old Bank House Cafe for a spot of breakfast before continuing on down the coast.

Afternoon

- Visit Inchydoney Beach, Skibbereen and of course the most southern point of the Island Mizen Head and Fastnet Lighthouse where you will have plenty of photo opportunities.

- Continue on towards Kenmare where you will stay this evening.

Westport, Co. Mayo (commons.wikimedia.org)

Evening

- We recommend heading out to PF Mccarthy's Bar & Restaurant for some dinner and drinks this evening.

Day 3

Morning/Afternoon

- Drive to Killarney and spend the next two days exploring the area in and around Killarney City and Killarney National Park.

- Make sure to take the tour of Muckross House, visit Torc Waterfall, Ross Castle.

Evening

- Grab a pizza and locally brewed beer at Killarney Brewing Company.

Day 4

Morning/Afternoon

- Grab a lovely breakfast at Cafe du Parc to set you up for your day of adventure around the areas near Killarney.

- Venture off to Molls Gap, Gap of Dunloe, Kenmare or Portmagee (for ferries to Skellig Islands and land bridge to Valentia Island).

- Spend the afternoon either on the islands or on the mainland.

Evening

- Grab a few pints and some Irish pub grub in The Dingle Pub, a local favourite, and if you fancy trying some locally brewed beer, make your way to Dick Mack's Brewhouse or Dingle Distillery if you are a whiskey connoisseur.

Day 6

Morning/Afternoon

- Set yourself up for the 3 hour drive towards Lahinch today with breakfast at Bean in Dingle.

- Stop off at the famous Cliffs of Moher, which tower 120 metres above the Atlantic Ocean. Be cautious here as the wind can be quite strong and protection from the edge is limited.

Evening

- Arriving in Lahinch, spend the evening dining at Barrtra Seafood restaurant, followed by drinks and live music at Lahinch Tavern and Grill, which you can alternatively choose to have dinner at.

Eyre Square, Co. Galway (commons.wikimedia.org)

Day 7

Morning

- Drive 2 and a half hours to Westport, County Mayo where you can explore this beautiful colourful town.

- You need to stop in at Cupan Tae, a traditional tea room with some amazing homemade treats and a great sit down morning tea experience.

Afternoon

- Drive towards Westport Harbour, which is a short ten minute drive from the town centre.

- Stop off at one of the quayside restaurants for some lunch and sensational ocean views.

- You can continue on to either gaze upon or hike Croagh Patrick, Ireland's famous holy mountain.

Evening

- Enjoy some dinner at JJ O Malleys Bar and Restaurant, followed by a visit to Matt Molloy's pub, one of the most famous in the town, for being owned by Matt Molloy the former Chieftains member.

Day 8

Morning/Afternoon

- Today, you will continue north along the Wild Atlantic Way towards the bustling surf town of Bundoran, which was named by the *National Geographic* as one of the world's Top 20 surf towns in 2012.

- Take your time along the coast here, and make sure to stop for photos along the way. Bring a hot flask of tea with some amazing homemade treats and enjoy this great sit down morning tea experience.

- Have some brunch or lunch at The Salty Fox when you arrive in Bundoran.

Evening

- Have a lovely dinner at Maddens Bridge Bar, followed by an evening of live music at Bundoran's best music venue, Grand Central Bundoran.

Day 9

Morning

- From Bundoran, you will make your way back south on The Wild Atlantic Way towards Galway City, a two and a half hour drive.

Afternoon

- Take the afternoon to explore Galway City by foot including the medieval streets, Spanish Arch and Eyre Square.

Evening

- Enjoy a traditional dinner in the Latin Quarter by night at The Front Door and Sonny's Bar and Restaurant.

- Stay the night at your chosen accommodation.

Day 10

Morning

- On your last day, you can spend the morning exploring more of Galway City as you please or take the walk to Salthill for some fresh sea air before the two and a half hour drive back to Cork.

Afternoon

- Take the drive back to Cork, stopping at Bunratty Castle along the way.

Evening

- Upon arrival back in Cork, head out for some dinner and drinks at the award winning restaurant Holy Smoke for your final night of the trip.

- If you are vegetarian, we highly recommend having dinner at the ever popular Cafe Paradiso, located on the quays.

The Rock of Cashel, Co. Tipperary (commons.wikimedia.org)

Day 1-2

- Pick up your car in Dublin and spend the next two days exploring Dublin City and all its sights including, Dublin Castle, Trinity College, Stephens Green.

- Perhaps spend Day 2 on a DART trip along the coast stopping at some of the seaside towns.

- Make sure to take a tour of the Guinness Storehouse to learn about the black stuff and pour a pint of your own and the Jameson Distillery, to learn about our famous whiskey.

- Stay two nights at your preferred accommodation.

Insider Tip: If you don't fancy walking around the city, take a hop on hop off bus, as driving in the city is not recommended both because of traffic and parking issues. This is the best option to see everything in a short time and leave the stress behind.

Day 3

Morning

- Drive to Kilkenny to check out Kilkenny Castle, and stroll around the many colourful winding streets.

Afternoon

- Take a trip out to Mt Juliet Estate and take a stroll around the quaint town of Thomastown, home to a huge amount of pubs for such a small place.

Evening

- Stay the night in Kilkenny at your preferred accommodation.

- Have dinner at The Left Bank, a great place which has won many awards and is just a minutes walk from the castle.

- Have a few pints at Kytelers Inn, dating back to 1324, making it one of the oldest inns in the country.

Day 4

Morning

- Continue on to Cork with a stop off at The Rock of Cashel and Hore Abbey, a 13th-century monastery that you must see.

Dingle Peninsula, Co. Kerry (ireland.com)

Afternoon/Evening

- This afternoon, make a stop at Blarney Castle to kiss the Blarney Stone, before reaching Cork.

- Stay the night in Cork City at your preferred accommodation.

- Check out some live music this evening at The Oliver Plunkett.

Day 5

Morning

- Spend the morning visiting the beautiful region of West Cork including, the towns of Kinsale, Clonakilty, Skibbereen and Glengarriff.

Afternoon

- Continue to Killarney where you will have the afternoon to explore the town and surrounding areas.

Evening

- Grab a delicious pizza and beer at Killarney Brewing Company before heading back into the town for some live music at The Killarney Grand.

- Stay two nights at your preferred accommodation.

Day 6

Morning/Afternoon

- Grab some breakfast first at The Shire Cafe, before your day of exploring begins.

- Today can be spent venturing further into Killarney National Park to visit the historic sights and nature trails here.

- Enjoy a delicious afternoon tea at Muckross Hotel and Spa for a delightful and luxurious treat.

Evening

- This evening, try some unique cocktails at The Lane Cafe Bar or for a more traditional evening, grab a pint at John M Reidys, a quirky pub with a sweet shop shopfront.

- Spend your second night at your preferred accommodation in Killarney.

Blarney Castle, Co. Cork (commons.wikimedia.org)

Day 7

Morning

- From Killarney, drive an hour to the Dingle Peninsula and spend the morning exploring Dingle town and the coastline of the peninsula.

Afternoon

- Have some fish and chips at Dingle Ahoy to get yourself ready for a bit of driving and adventuring up the coast.

- Drive north to the Cliffs of Moher, a three hour drive from Dingle, where you can observe the famous steep cliffs of Ireland that continue to attract people every year.

Evening

- Head to Gus O'Connor's for some dinner and drinks this evening.

Day 8

Morning

- Today, you will have a relatively short drive of one and a half hours to reach Galway where you will have the chance to explore the city itself, and the surrounding areas of Spiddal and Salthill.

Afternoon

- We recommend driving further out to the coast this afternoon, where you can visit the popular towns of Roundstone and Clifden.

Evening

- Enjoy some dinner and drinks in the city and stay one night here at your preferred accommodation.

- Head to the Latin Quarter, for a great choice of restaurants and live music options.

Day 9

Morning

- This morning, make your way towards Athlone for the night.

- Make sure to visit Athlone Castle and Derryglad Folk and Heritage Museum.

The Muckross Hotel & Spa , Co. Killarney (commons.wikimedia.org)

Afternoon

Make a stop off at Lough Ree, the largest lake on the River Shannon, for a bit of peace and tranquillity and of course, great photo opportunities.

Evening

- Hatters Lane Bistro is a must for a unique dinner this evening in Athlone.

- Have a pint in Sean's Bar, Ireland's (and possibly the world's) oldest pub, dating back to 900AD.

Day 10

Morning

- Spend the morning exploring Athlone.

Athlone Castle , Co. Athlone (commons.wikimedia.org)

Afternoon

- Continue on to Dublin to catch up on the sights you missed and grab a late lunch or early dinner of delicious fish and chips at the famous Beshoffs Bros chip shop.

Evening

- Head to Whelans for some live music this evening and some drinks for your final night of the trip.

- Stay one night at your preferred accommodation.

14 Day Itinerary: Two Week Roller-Coastal

Belfast, Donegal, Sligo, Mayo, Galway

Day 1-2

- Pick up your car at Belfast airport or Belfast City and spend the next two days exploring Belfast City.

- Highlights in the city include the Titanic Museum located in the Titanic Quarter where you will see Harland and Wolff, two of the largest dry docks in Europe and where the famous Titanic was built in 1909.

- Don't miss out on Crumlin Road Gaol if you are not afraid of paranormal happenings, Falls Road, The Peace Wall, The Ulster Museum and the many bars, restaurants and shopping areas too.

- Driving in any city can be stressful and Belfast is no exception so perhaps you can opt for a walking tour or a hop on hop off tour of the city.

- Dining options for Belfast include, The Dock for delicious breakfast or lunch, as well as The Lantern for an amazing dinner.

- Stay two nights in Belfast at your preferred accommodation.

Day 3

Morning/Afternoon

- Make your way north to begin your trip along the Causeway Coast, beginning with a stop off at the *Game of Thrones* locations such as Carnlough Harbour, Caves of Cushendun, The Dark Hedges and Ballintoy Harbour before continuing on to stay the night in Bushmills. Even if you are not a *G.O.T* fan, these spots are still worth stopping at.

- When you arrive in Bushmills, take a tour of the Bushmills Distillery, which draws 120,000 visitors every year.

Evening

- Try out The Porthole Bar and Restaurant for dinner followed by drinks at The Bushmills Inn.

Day 4

Morning/Afternoon

- Today you will spend time at the UNESCO World Heritage Site of The Giant's Causeway and Carrick-a-Rede Rope Bridge, a quick ten minute drive from Bushmills.

- The 40,000 interlocking basalt columns are very impressive, and you will understand why people venture from all over the world to see this phenomenon.

- Take your time here enjoying the view and the visitor centre, before making your way back to Bushmills for another night at your preferred accommodation.

- If you have time on return to Bushmills check out the Bushmills Visitor Centre, Dunseverick Castle and Dunseverick Falls.

Evening

- Tonight, we recommend to treat yourself to dinner and drinks at The Tartine Restaurant at The Distillers Arms.

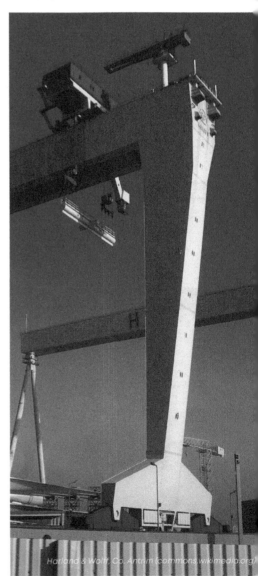

Harland & Wolff, Co. Antrim (commons.wikimedia.org)

Day 5

Morning

- Today, you will cross the border into the Republic of Ireland, so don't forget to pay attention to the speed limits, which will now be written in kilometres. Don't get caught out!

- You will enter the county of Donegal which is famous for so many reasons, mainly its natural, wild beauty, its world renowned surf beaches and its islands, one of which you will venture off to today.

Afternoon

- Arriving two and a half hours from Bushmills to Burtonport, County Donegal, you will take the car ferry to the island of Arranmore.

- This is an enchanted island which is wild and untamed and full of culture. An absolute must see when in the region.

- Here, you can opt to take on some hikes, check out the dramatic caves, sandy beaches or try some water activities in the perfect waters surrounding the island. The Gaelic traditions are alive and well here so this will be an experience to remember.

Evening

- Spend the evening at the island's favourite bar, Early's pub, for drinks and traditional Irish music.

Day 6

Morning/Afternoon

- Upon arrival back to the mainland, drive one and a half hours south to the popular surf town of Bundoran, which has been a summer holiday destination for Irish people for decades.

- This Blue Flag beach is one of many in the country, in fact Donegal has the longest coastline and the most Blue Flag beaches in the country, so if you are a beach lover, you will love Donegal and Bundoran.

- Don't miss out on having a coffee or some lunch at the award winning Buoys and Gulls Coffee this afternoon.

Evening

- Enjoy an evening of live music at Grand Central Donegal.

- Dining options for dinner include the ever popular Maddens Bridge Bar and McGarrigles Restaurant.

- Stay at your preferred accommodation tonight.

Carrick a Rede Rope Bridge, Co. Antrim (commons.wikimedia.org)

Day 7

Morning/Afternoon

- Drive a short forty minutes along the surf coast to Strandhill, County Sligo, where you will have the opportunity to gaze out at the brave surfers tacking the big Atlantic waves, or even try your hand at surfing from one of the many surf schools.

- You can explore the hills of the region, go kayaking, visit the Strandhill people's market, try some golf or relax at the Voya Seaweed Baths in the afternoon. The choices are endless.

- Shells cafe is the perfect choice for a coffee or spot of lunch or brunch.

Evening

- Have dinner this evening at The Strand Bar and maybe even pop into Mammy Johnston's Ice Cream Parlour for a dessert treat before heading to the pub for some pints.

- Stay one night here in Strandhill.

Day 8-9

- After breakfast at Shells Cafe, drive two and a half hours to Achill Island located in County Mayo and connected by land bridge, so no ferries are needed.

- Here, you will spend two days enjoying traditional island life, either by bicycle or by car.

- The scenery is fantastic so take your time and be prepared to stop a lot for photos.

- On either evening have some dinner at Teds Pub, and enjoy live music at The Annexe Inn.

- Don't forget to stop off at Lynott's Pub,

either for a daytime pint or evening mingle with the locals in this traditional thatched island pub.

- This island, the largest of all islands off the coast of Ireland is stepped in history and you will see this by visiting the Deserted Village which dates back to early Medieval times.

- Visit Keem Bay for a fantastic view, especially at the top of the hill as you drive down towards the beach.

- The roads on Achill Island are very narrow and some are steep, so drive slowly and carefully.

- Stay two nights at your preferred accommodation.

Strandhill People's Market Co. Sligo (facebook.com)

Day 10-11

- Today, you will return to the mainland and stay two nights in Westport, a vibrant town full of history, great food and welcoming people.

- Don't miss afternoon tea at Cupan Tae, a drive to Westport Harbour, a hike to Croagh Patrick and a coastal drive along Clew Bay.

- Spend an evening at Matt Molloys, the most famous pub in Westport, for a pint. It is owned by the famous Chieftains member, Matt Molloy, and is the best place for traditional music any night of the week.

- Stay at your preferred accommodation for two nights.

Achill Island, Co. Mayo (commons.wikimedia.org)

Day 12

Morning/Afternoon

- Take the coast route by making your way to the beautiful town of Roundstone.

- From here you will have the opportunity to explore the areas around the Connemara region such as the towns of Spiddal, Clifden and of course the majestic Connemara National Park.

- Be sure to stop for a local seafood lunch at Ardagh Restaurant.

Evening

- Spend the evening in the neighbouring town of Clifden enjoying drinks and live music at the award winning Lowry's Bar, which has Connemara's largest selection of premium whiskey and gin.

Day 13

Morning/Afternoon

- This morning, take the two and a half hour drive to Carrick on Shannon as you slowly make your way back to Belfast.

- This is the cruising capital of the River Shannon, so be sure to hop aboard one of the many river cruises.

- If you fancy seeing the smallest chapel in the country, you can visit Costello Chapel located in the heart of the town, and it measures at just 4.8 metres x 3.6 metres.

Evening

- Enjoy dinner at The Red Bank Restaurant and drinks/live music at Cryans Bar, which is known as the Matt Molloys of Carrick on Shannon. If you fancy exploring more pubs, try out the popular Dunnes Bar for a pint or two.

Day 14

Morning/Afternoon

- Today, make your way back to Belfast, a journey of about two and a half hours.

- This afternoon, stop off at Lough Neagh, the largest lake in the British Isles.

Evening

- Head to The Empire this evening for some great music at Belfast's favourite music venue.

- Grab some dinner at Holohans at The Barge tonight.

- Stay one night here at your preferred accommodation.

14 Day Itinerary: The Ultimate Two Weeker

Dublin, Meath, Belfast, Donegal, Sligo, Mayo, Galway, Kerry, Kilkenny

Day 1-2

- Pick up your car in Dublin and spend the next two days exploring the bustling capital and all its wonderful, historical sights.

- It's best to leave the car at the hotel and either venture off on foot, or on public transport (such as the LUAS tram, Dublin Bus or DART train). These are all great ways to see the coastline of Dublin Bay.

- There are plenty of dining and pub options throughout the guide, so you will not miss out on a great night out in the city.

- Stay two nights at your preferred accommodation here in Dublin.

Day 3

Morning/Afternoon

- Make your way towards Newgrange in County Meath, which is a short forty minute drive away.

- This impressive passage tomb is a national attraction you must not miss, considering it is older than both Stonehenge and The Pyramids of Giza.

Holohans at The Barge, Co. Antrim facebook.com

Evening

- From here, continue north to Belfast City where you will stay for two nights at your preferred accommodation.

- There are many restaurants, bars and music venues highlighted in the guide, so you have many options for the evening here in the city.

Day 4-5

- The drive from Newgrange to Belfast is just an hour and a half, and once again, don't forget the signs will change to miles per hour once you get over the border.

- You will stay two nights here to really get to know the city and surroundings, but of course all itineraries can be modified so feel free to stay an extra night anywhere along the way.

- Make sure to visit all the major attractions including, the Peace Wall, the paranormal prison of Crumlin Road Gaol, Titanic Museum and Falls Rd.

- A hop on hop off bus tour is recommended here, because Belfast has such a deep and extensive history, so it's best not to miss out on the backstories of what you're seeing.

- Dining and pub options are listed in previous itineraries, so make sure to try the various suggestions.

Day 6

Morning

- From Belfast, it is a short drive north towards the Causeway Coast, where you can opt to stop at the *Game of Thrones* locations, listed in previous itineraries.

Afternoon

- Continue on towards The Giant's Causeway and Carrick-a-Rede Rope Bridge, located close to the town of Bushmills.

- In Bushmills we recommend you do a distillery tour at the Bushmills Distillery dating back to 1708, which is one of the most famous distilleries in the world.

Evening

- Spend the night in Bushmills at your preferred accommodation.

- See previous itineraries for great restaurant and live music ideas in Bushmills.

Dublin City, Co. Dublin (commons.wikimedia.org)

Day 7

Morning/Afternoon

- On your way to Bundoran, stop off for the night in Derry officially known as Londonderry, the town where the popular comedy *Derry Girls* is set.

- Here you should definitely explore the 17th-century city walls, visit the Tower Museum to see the infamous 16th-century shipwrecks and view the city from the Peace Bridge as well as take a walking tour to explore the city's vibrant murals.

- Stop at Pyke N Pommes for a quick bite to eat or some coffee as you explore the city.

Evening

- This evening go for some dinner at The Sooty Olive Restaurant, followed by an evening at Peadar O'Donnell's Bar, where you will be sure to have a crowd around you, as this is a popular spot for the live music and atmosphere.

Insider Tip: Derry, is located where the Causeway Coast and the Wild Atlantic Way meet, so this is a great spot to explore both coastal touring routes.

Day 8

Morning/Afternoon

- Take a one and a half hour drive from Bushmills to the atmospheric surf town of Bundoran, where there are many surf schools offering lessons as well as the famous Roguey cliff walk, West End Walk and Bundoran Fairy Bridges, a must see hidden gem of Ireland.

- Stay the night in Bundoran.

Day 9 - 10

- Day 9 you will take a leisurely drive to Galway City, stopping off at the surf beach of Strandhill in County Sligo.

- Continue to the pilgrimage town of Knock, County Mayo, where people have been visiting for years since the holy apparition in 1879.

- Upon arrival, check into your hotel where you'll stay for two nights, and explore The City of Tribes by foot.

- Spend Day 10 visiting the coastal towns of Spiddal, Roundstone and Clifden and spend the evening listening to live music in Galway City.

Giants Causeway, Co. Antrim (commons.wikimedia.org)

Day 11-12

- Your journey will take you further south today towards Killarney, a two and a half hour drive, where you have two days to explore.

- En route you will stop off at Bunratty Castle, the famous 15th-century tower house close to Shannon.

- Take another detour to explore Adare Manor, this Neo-Gothic architectural masterpiece which is now a hotel and golf resort. If you are feeling like a treat, drop by the spa for some relaxing treatments.

- Upon arrival in Killarney, you will probably be tired, so you can take an easy afternoon. In the evening, enjoy some dinner and drinks at suggestions previously mentioned in the guide, before spending the next day exploring the city and surrounding national park fully.

- Take a tour of Muckross House, which has an amazing history, followed by a walk around the beautiful gardens.

- Check out Killarney Brewing Company, the first of its kind in Ireland, featuring an in house brewery and pizzeria, before spending the second night here in Killarney.

- Stay at your preferred accommodation both nights here in Killarney.

Day 13

Morning

- For your last full day, you will have a two hour and forty five minute drive towards Kilkenny, with a stop off at The Rock of Cashel, located in County Tipperary.

Afternoon

- In Kilkenny, you can explore the impressive castle and its grounds as well as Black Abbey and St Canices Cathedral, not forgetting the many pubs and restaurants to check out too.

Evening

- Check out previous itineraries for some evening inspiration, including The Left Bank pub for a great evening out in the city.

- Stay tonight in Kilkenny at your preferred accommodation.

Bunratty Castle, Co. Clare (commons.wikimedia.org)

Day 14

- Depending on when you need to drop the car back to Dublin, you can leave early or choose to spend the morning in Kilkenny, as it is a short one hour and a half drive back to the capital.

- Upon arrival in Dublin, you can spend the afternoon as you please, before enjoying your last night of the trip at one of Temple Bar's best pubs, The Temple Bar.

- Stay tonight in Dublin at your preferred accommodation.

Insider Tip: It's worth noting that the toll roads will speed up the time, but if you have time to kill, avoid the tolls and take the N roads. There may be a few R roads, if you choose to go off the beaten track, so beware that in Ireland these can be very narrow, windy and some even without signposts, so take your time.

Killarney Brewing Co., Co. Kerry (facebook.com)

21 Day Itinerary: The Big Daddy Coastal Route

Cork to Cork Loop

Day 1-2

- Begin your trip in Cork, where you can spend the first two days exploring the city before venturing off the following day to the quirky colourful town of Cobh, where the Titanic set sail in 1912.

- There is a Titanic museum here, which is located in the heart of the town, and is worth a visit.

- Highlights to see in the city include Cork City Gaol, The English Market and Blackrock Castle.

- There are many dining options as well as music and pub suggestions throughout this guidebook so feel free to try as many as you can while you are here.

- Stay in Cork for two nights at your preferred accommodation.

Day 3

Morning/Afternoon

- Leave Cork City and take a drive through the beautiful region of West Cork, specifically the towns of Kinsale, Clonakilty, Skibbereen and Glengarriff.

- Have a lovely seafood lunch in Clifden at Ardagh Restaurant.

Evening

- Head to the Blue Loo Pub this evening for a traditional West Cork experience.

Day 4

Morning

- Before leaving Glengariff, you can take the ferry to Garnish Island which is famed for its manicured gardens. Have some coffee and a tasty treat at The Garnish Cafe this morning before continuing on.

Afternoon

- Continue onwards towards Killarney where you can spend the day exploring Killarney National Park, with its many attractions, listed in previous itineraries.

Evening

- Make your way back to Killarney for some pub grub at The Laurels Pub. From here, the options are endless for a night on the town, or alternatively a few pints with the locals.

- Stay one night in Killarney, at your preferred accommodation.

Day 5

Morning/Afternoon

- Today, you will leave Killarney and drive the Ring of Kerry, stopping off at the towns of Kenmare, Caherdaniel,Waterville, Portmagee and onwards to Killorglin.

- Take the optional ferry from Portmagee to visit the ever popular Skellig Islands or take the land bridge to visit Valentia Island, where you will spend the afternoon.

Evening

- Have a delicious dinner at the Bianconi Restaurant this evening.

Day 6

Morning/Afternoon

- Today, you will drive from Killorglin to Dingle, a short forty five minute drive, where you can spend the day exploring the Dingle Peninsula.

- Stay one night in Dingle at your preferred accommodation.

Evening

- Evening options for Dingle are listed in previous itineraries, so be sure not to miss out on our suggestions.

Killarney National Park , Co. Kerry (commons.wikimedia.org)

Day 7

Morning

- From Dingle, make your way north to the town of Tralee a short forty minutes away, well known for its long standing Irish pageant, The Rose of Tralee.

Afternoon

- Check out the Kerry County Museum this afternoon, an award-winning museum located in the Ashe Memorial Hall, as well as Blennerville Windmill.

- Stroll through Tralee town park, one of Ireland's largest green areas as well as spending a couple of hours at Siamsa Tire National Folk Theatre for a cultural experience to remember.

- Enjoy some lunch at 7th Heaven Bistro and Cafe this afternoon.

Lahinch, Co. Clare (commons.wikimedia.org)

Evening

- Try Quinlans Seafood Bar this evening for some local seafood, followed by drinks at Turner's Lounge, which also doubles as a gastropub, if you fancy having dinner here.

- Enjoy live music at The Brogue Inn.

Day 8

Morning/Afternoon

- After a morning in Tralee town, drive two hours to the surf town of Lahinch in County Clare for a relaxing break away.

- This is an adventure hub so if this is your thing, you have many things to keep you busy including surfing, indoor climbing, kayaking, archery and golf.

- On the other hand if you prefer to relax, take a stroll along Lahinch Beach and Lahinch promenade as well as browse the local shops.

Evening

- Tonight, you must spend the evening at Lahinch Tavern and Grill enjoying dinner and live music seven nights a week, something West Clare is known for.

- Stay a night at your preferred accommodation.

Day 9

- Today, you will take the two hour drive to Westport, County Mayo, opting to extend the drive by stopping at spots along the way such as Doolin, Kinvarra.

- You can also opt to take a more direct inland route through Athenry which will take you along N and M roads, but the coastal route will have much smaller and windier roads, but with spectacular views of the Wild Atlantic Way.

Be prepared to spend the day stopping at places that grab your attention and browsing shops in the small coastal towns. Take it all in and take your time, before arriving in Westport for a relaxing evening.

Day 10

On your second day in Westport, spend the morning exploring the colourful streets of the town, browsing the local stores and in the afternoon, take a drive out to Westport Harbour for a different perspective.

Drive along the coast to get views of Clew Bay, Croagh Patrick and pass

Roundstone , Co. Galway (commons.wikimedia.org)

through some tiny villages eventually coming to the Famine Ship Memorial Monument, which is worth a quick stop off.

- On your way back, opt to take the hike to Croagh Patrick, or even walk around the grounds, alternatively continue back to the town and visit Westport House and Gardens.

- Stay two nights at your preferred accommodation in Westport and don't miss out on our evening suggestions listed earlier in the guidebook.

Day 11

Morning

- This morning, take the short drive over the Michael Davitt Bridge towards Achill Island, the largest island off of Ireland.

- Here you will get the chance to experience real Irish culture, as told by the islanders.

- This island has so much history and the locals are forever working to keep the traditions alive, including the language and way of life.

Afternoon

- Visit the deserted village, Keem Bay, Keel Beach, Achill Experience Aquarium and Visitor Centre, Kildavnet Castle and Achill Heritage Centre.

Evening

- Enjoy some pub grub and some pints in Mickey's pub or Gielty's pub this evening.

Day 12

Morning

- Take the two hour drive towards Bundoran, stopping off at Strandhill beach to watch the surfers and take a stroll along the promenade.

- Grab some breakfast or a coffee at Shells Cafe before continuing to Bundoran.

Afternoon

- In the afternoon, opt for some surf lessons at one of the best destinations in the world for surfing. There are many surf schools to choose from and you'll be in good hands here.

Evening

- Grab some well deserved pub grub after a day of adventure at The Phoenix Tavern, followed by some drinks at Brennan's pub.

Day 13

Morning/Afternoon

- From Bundoran, you will continue towards the town of Derry aka Londonderry which is steeped in history and will give you a better understanding of 'The Troubles' in Ireland and Northern Ireland.

- The Walled City has many things to see and do including visiting The Walled City Brewery, the city murals, the city walls and the Bloody Sunday memorial.

Evening

- Bennigans Bar and Jazz Club is on the agenda tonight after dinner at The Shipquay Restaurant.

- Stay one night at your preferred accommodation.

Insider Tip: You will cross the border to Northern Ireland so once again be aware of the road signs changing from kilometres to miles and the rules of the road may vary. As well as this, you have to walk the city walls here, because it is the only city in Ireland to still have these intact and it is one of the best examples in all of Europe. To get to know more about the city and its history go to the Free Derry Museum, The Tower Museum and The Siege Museum.

Bundoran, Co. Donegal (commons.wikimedia.org)

Day 14

Morning/Afternoon

- Make your way from Derry to the town of Bushmills.

- Staying a night in Bushmills town is key on an Irish road trip as it is famous for its whiskey and as being a great base for visiting The Giant's Causeway, this is a stop off you cannot miss.

Evening

- You will stay the night, after plenty of whiskey tasting, so take your time and enjoy each sip.

- Stay at your preferred accommodation and don't miss out on evening options for dining and music, listed in previous itineraries.

Day 15-16

- The drive from Bushmills to Belfast is only an hour, the quickest route, but should you fancy stopping at the film locations for *Game of Thrones*, it will add a bit more distance and time to your route, but will be worth it.

- Key stop offs are Cushendun, Dunluce Castle and Carnlough.

- Stay two nights in Belfast City at your preferred accommodation.

- On the first afternoon you can explore the city and its traditional pubs and on the following day, tick off all the major sights, listed earlier on in previous itineraries.

Day 17

Morning/Afternoon

- Belfast and Dublin are not as far apart as you may think and with the new roads, it takes under two hours from city to city.

- You will have two days to discover Dublin and its surroundings so take your time as you drive south from Belfast, perhaps detouring to Newgrange Heritage Site and the town of Drogheda, if you wish.

- As you are entering Dublin from the north, why not stop off at Howth Pier for a walk and for some famous fish and chips at Beshoffs. If the weather allows, take the Howth Cliff walk for beautiful views out into Dublin Bay.

Dublin Castle, Co. Dublin (commons.wikimedia.org)

Evening

- Spend the first evening soaking up the atmosphere in one of the many pubs in Temple Bar. Prices here are always more expensive than anywhere else in the city so if you are on a budget, grab some dinner and drinks outside of the main area.

- Stay two nights at your preferred accommodation.

Day 18

Morning/Afternoon

- The next day you have the whole day to visit all the sites of the city including Kilmainham Gaol, Guinness Storehouse, Jameson Distillery, Dublin Castle, Grafton Street, St Stephen's Green and of course the quirky cobbled streets of Temple Bar by day.

Evening

- Why not check out a musical at the Bord Gais Theatre on one of your evenings in Dublin?

Day 19

Morning

- You will have a short forty minute drive to Waterford today so feel free to take the morning to visit more of Dublin before continuing on.

Afternoon

- You can opt to detour to the town of Thomastown, home of the impressive Mount Juliet Estate.

- In Waterford City visit the main sights which are located within the Viking Triangle, once controlled by the Viking city walls.

- Reginald's Tower, Bishops Place and Waterford Treasures Medieval Museum are impressive places to visit in the city.

Evening

- Head to Uluru, for a unique dining experience as well as some drinks.

Day 20

Morning

- On your second day, you can venture further afield to the town of Tramore, where you can grab some coffee at Tra Coffee Roasters.

- Tramore is a bustling summer destination for Irish people, which features a beautiful stretch of beach, Lafcadio Hearn Japanese Gardens and of course Tramore Amusement Park. If you are travelling with small kids, this will be a great day out for everyone.

Tramore , Co. Waterford (commons.wikimedia.org)

Afternoon

If you fancy something a little bit more relaxing and authentic, head to the small town of Fethard on Sea on the Hook Peninsula, in Ireland's 'sunniest corner'.

This is a great place to take in the beautiful rural scenery, stroll the village and grab a pint and some lunch at the ever so traditional McCarthy's pub.This will be a real Irish experience and a great way to spend the afternoon.

Evening

Make your way back to Waterford City for some dinner and drink and check out the old school pub of Jack Meades too.

Fethard , Co Wexford (commons.wikimedia.org)

Day 21

Morning/Afternoon

- On your way back to Cork to drop off the car, take the coastal route, stopping off at Dungarvan, Youghal and Middleton.

Evening

- Stay the night at your preferred accommodation in Cork, and check out previous itineraries for some nightlife options in the city.

21 Day Itinerary: The Full Monty

Dublin, Kilkenny, Cork, Killarney, Galway, Sligo, Belfast

Day 1-3

- Fly into Dublin and after a few days exploring the sights of the city, hire your car on the day you plan to leave. Highlights are listed in all previous itineraries featuring Dublin as a stop off.

- A rental car won't be needed in the city, so best to take a hop on hop off, walk in the city centre or take public transport which will save you money.

- The DART will take you to many coastal towns and LUAS and Dublin Bus will take you all around the city and to the commuter towns too.

- Be sure to thoroughly check our suggestions throughout the guidebook, not to miss out on the best dining options and nightlife in Dublin.

Day 4

Morning/Afternoon

- Hire your car this morning and take the drive to Glendalough and Roundwood for a date with nature amongst The Wicklow Mountains before arriving in Kilkenny.

Evening

- Stay tonight in Kilkenny at your preferred accommodation and check out evening options in our previous itineraries.

Day 5-6

Morning/Afternoon

- Drive from Kilkenny to Waterford via a stop off at the Rock of Cashel and stay two nights in the Viking City of Waterford.

- Explore the areas between the Viking Triangle over your two day stay in the city.

- Grab some dinner and pints one of the evenings at Jack Meades Bar, for a real local experience.

Day 7

Morning

- Today, you will have the option to stop at Dungarvan, Youghal and Middleton on your way to Kinsale, County Cork, so take your time exploring the region, before arriving in West Cork.

Afternoon

- Spend the rest of the afternoon exploring the beautiful town of Kinsale, complete with its colorful houses.

- Have lunch at Toddies at the Bulman.

Evening

- Stay tonight in the quirky town of Kinsale and check out Armada Bar for an evening of live music and drinks.

Day 8

Morning/Afternoon

- From Kinsale, you will continue to Kenmare where you will stay the night at your preferred accommodation.

- In Kenmare, you can spend the morning and afternoon exploring the surrounding area and in particular The Ring of Beara peninsula.

Evening

- In Kenmare, head to Foleys for some amazing local food, and stop by Crowleys for the craic agus ceol.

Kenmare , Co. Kerry (commons.wikimedia.org

Day 9 - 12

The Ring of Kerry is on your to do list today (Day 9), so leave early to give yourself time to stop along the way for many photo opportunities. You will need extra time too if you plan to drive to Valentia Island or take the ferry from Portmagee to Skellig Michael.

Tonight, you will stay in the village of Dingle, the only village on the Dingle Peninsula.

On your agenda today (Day 10) will be the coastal drive known as The Slea Head Loop.

The loop is about four or five hours starting and finishing in Dingle, but take caution at Slea Head as the road narrows a lot and can be challenging for oncoming traffic.

On your last full day in Dingle (Day 12), take the ferry from Ventry to the Great Blasket Islands which are full of history.

If you're lucky you will spot dolphins, minke whales and basking sharks on your ferry to the islands.

You will stay all three nights in Dingle at your preferred location, a great base for the surrounding areas.

Be sure to look back at previous itineraries for some evening inspiration and optional activities and dining options.

Day 13 - 14

- From Dingle, head north and you will arrive at The Cliffs of Moher, County Clare, an absolute must see and one of the top attractions in Ireland.

- On your second day (Day 14) in Galway, take the ferry from Rossaveal to the Aran Islands.

- You will spend these two nights in Galway City at your preferred accommodation.

Day 15

Morning/Afternoon

- The region of Connemara is located in County Galway and is a hub for Irish tradition and this is where you will spend the day.

- The language is alive and well here, and many students spend summers at the Gaeltacht here in the region to learn Irish, each year.

- Today, you will have the whole day to explore the area on your way to Westport.

Connemara national park, Co. Galway (commons. wikimedia.org)

Evening

- Upon arrival in Westport, check into your preferred accommodation and head to Matt Molloy's for a traditional pint.

Day 16

Morning/Afternoon

- The next few days will be spent in Northern Ireland, first stop in the town of Derry, where you can learn about the history of the city with the many museums and wall murals around the area.

Evening

- You will spend this evening in Derry and be sure to try the beer tasting at the Walled City Brewery, the only one of its kind in Northern Ireland.

- Spend the night at your preferred accommodation in Derry.

Day 17

Morning

- Take some extra time today to explore Derry, grabbing a morning coffee at The Coffee Tree.

Afternoon

- Take the drive towards Portrush, the small seaside resort town, where you can spend the afternoon, relaxing and unwinding at the beach.

Evening

- This evening, we highly recommend dinner and drinks with live music at The Atlantic Bar, the best place for live music in Portrush.

Day 18

- On your second day in Portrush, take your time to spend the day exploring the beautiful Antrim Coast which has been dedicated as an area of outstanding beauty since 1988.

- Here, you can stop off at the Glens of Antrim, The Giant's Causeway and a series of seaside villages.

Giants Causeway, Co. Antrim (commons.wikimedia.org)

Day 19

Morning

- From Portrush, you will drive to Belfast, the capital city of Northern Ireland.

Afternoon

- Spend the afternoon discovering the sights of the city including The Titanic Quarter, Queen's University, Crumlin Road Gaol and much more.

- The Titanic Museum is highly recommended to give you a great view and understanding of the story of one of the most famous ship disasters in history.

Evening

- Take some inspiration from our previous Belfast itineraries, whether it is live music, pub grub or a romantic night out you're after.

- Spend the night at your preferred accommodation here in the city.

Day 20

Morning/Afternoon

- You can opt to spend the morning finishing where you left off with your Belfast touring or continue on early to Boyne Valley located in County Meath, where you can take a step back in time, in this core area of Ireland's Ancient East region.

- Discover the Hill of Tara, Knowth and Dowth, Newgrange and of course Trim Castle, film location for the movie *Braveheart*.

- Have some lunch today at The Hill of Tara cafe, which serves up delicious homemade soups, sandwiches and scones.

Evening

- James Griffin pub has to be on the schedule tonight. This award winning pub has live trad sessions on Thursday, live bands on Friday/Sunday and DJs on Saturday.

- Tonight, you will stay in Trim, County Meath, at your preferred accommodation.

Day 21

Morning

- Today is your last full day so enjoy the town of Trim this morning, maybe stopping for breakfast at Harvest Home Bakery, before the drive back to Dublin.

Titanic Belfast, Co. Antrim (commons.wikimedia.org)

Afternoon

- Spend some time in Dublin, wandering around Georges Street Arcade and St Stephens Green Shopping Centre as well as browsing the shops around Grafton Street for souvenirs and gifts.

Evening

- This evening make a stop at The Porterhouse Brew Pub for some beer tasting and pub grub in a cosy yet casual atmosphere.

- Spend tonight at your preferred accommodation in Dublin.

St.Stephen's Green, Co. Dublin (commons.wikimedia.org)

The Extra Bits

Accommodation Options

Based on three types of budgets – affordable, mid-range and splashing out – these are our top picks for accommodation across the four provinces of Ireland.

Ulster

Affordable

Lagan Backpackers Belfast
Address: 121 Fitzroy Ave, Belfast, Co. Antrim

Premier Inn Derry
Address: Crescent Link, Co. Derry

Muldowney's Bed & Breakfast
Address: Upper, Illion, Aran Island, Co. Donegal

TurfnSurf Lodge and Surf School
Address: Upper, Illion, Aran Island, Co. Donegal

Mid-Range

Adelphi Portrush
Address: 67-71 Main St, Portrush, Co. Antrim

The Bayview Hotel
Address: 2 Bayhead Rd, Portballintrae, Bushmills, Co. Antrim

Malmaison Hotel

Address: 34-38 Victoria St, Belfast, Co. Antrim

Beech Hill Country House

Address: 32 Ardmore Rd, Co. Derry

Madden Bridge Bar and Guesthouse

Address: Main St, Magheracar, Bundoran, Co. Donegal

The Great Northern Hotel

Address: Sea Rd, Drumacrin, Bundoran, Co. Donegal

Splashing Out

Culloden Estate and Spa

Address: Bangor Rd, Holywood, Co. Antrim

Shipquay Hotel

Address: 15-17 Shipquay St, Co. Derry

Lough Erne Resort

Address: 193 Lough Shore Rd, Ross Inner, Enniskillen, Co. Fermanagh

Munster

Affordable

Aille River Hostel & Camping

Address: Ocean Road, Teergonean, Doolin, Co. Clare

Bru Bar Hostel

Address: 57 MacCurtain Street, Co. Cork

Ferry Boat Guesthouse

Address: Portmagee, Co. Kerry

Mid-Range

Lahinch Coast Hotel

Address: Station Rd, Crag, Lahinch, Co. Clare

Trident Hotel Kinsale

Address: Kinsale, Co. Cork

The Imperial Hotel

Address: 76 S Mall, Street, Co. Cork

Brook Lane Hotel

Address: Casey's, Killarney Road, Kenmare, Co. Kerry

Butler Arms Hotel

Address: Waterville, Co. Kerry

Malmaison Belfast, Co. Antrim

Dingle Skellig Hotel

Address: Farran, Dingle, Co. Kerry

Killarney Towers Hotel and Leisure Centre

Address: College St, Killarney, Co. Kerry

The Ashe Hotel

Address: Maine St, Tralee, Co. Kerry

Granville Hotel

Address: Meagher's Quay, Co. Waterford

The Majestic Hotel

Address: Tramore East, Tramore, Co. Waterford

Splashing Out

Fota Island Resort Hotel

Address: Fota Island, Co. Cork

Westport Plaza Hotel, Co. Mayo

Muckross Park House Hotel & Spa

Address: Muckross Rd, Killarney, Co. Kerry

Cliff House Hotel

Address: Middle Road, Dysert, Ardmore, Co. Waterford

Connaught

Affordable

Keel Sandybanks Camping

Address: Keel East, Achill Island, Co. Mayo

The Strand Hotel

Address: Doogort, Achill Island, Co. Mayo

The White House Hostel

Address: 4 Markievicz Rd, Rathquarter, Co. Sligo

Mid-Range

Aran Islands Hotel

Address: Kilronan, Aran Islands, Co. Galway

Foyles Hotel

Address: Main St, Clifden, Co. Galway

The House Hotel

Address: Spanish Parade, Latin Quarter, Co. Galway

Landmark Hotel

Address: Shannon Lodge, Townparks, Carrick-On-Shannon, Co. Leitrim

Westport Plaza Hotel

Address: Castlebar St, Carrowbeg, Westport, Co. Mayo

Achill Cliff House Hotel

Address: Keel, Achill Island, Co. Mayo

Yeats Country Hotel

Address: Rosses Upper, Rosses Point, Co. Sligo

Strandhill Lodge & Suites

Address: Top Rd, Larass, Strandhill, Co. Sligo

Splashing Out

The G Hotel and Spa

Address: Wellpark, The, Old Dublin Rd, Co. Galway

Ashford Castle

Address: Ashford Castle Drive, Leaf Island, Cong, Co. Mayo

Lough Key House

Address: Kilbryan, Boyle, Co. Roscommon

The G Hotel and Spa, Co. Galway

Leinster

Affordable

Generator Hostel

Address: Smithfield, Dublin 7, Co. Dublin

Lanigans Bar and Hostel

Address: 29 Rose Inn St, Gardens, Co. Kilkenny

Lough Crew Glamping

Address: Drumsawry, Oldcastle, Co. Meath

Mid-Range

Fitzsimons Hotel Temple Bar

Address: 21/22 Wellington Quay, Temple Bar, Co. Dublin

Grand Canal Hotel

Address: Grand Canal Street Upper, Co. Dublin

Marlin Hotel Dublin

Address: 11 Bow Ln E, St Stephen's Green, Co. Dublin

Hotel Kilkenny

Address: College Rd, Sugarloaf Hill, Co. Kilkenny

Boyne Valley Hotel

Address: Dublin Rd, Roschoill, Drogheda, Co. Louth

Knightsbrook Hotel and Spa

Address: Dublin Rd, Iffernock, Trim, Co. Meath

Dunbrody Country House Hotel

Address: Mersheen, Arthurstown, Co. Wexford

Summerhill House Hotel

Address: Enniskerry Demesne, Cookstown, Co. Wicklow

The Glenview Hotel and Leisure Club

Address: Glen of The Downs, Co. Wicklow

Woodenbridge Hotel and Lodge

Address: Vale of Avoca, Arklow, Co. Wicklow

Splashing Out

The Shelbourne Hotel

Address: 27 St Stephen's Green, Co. Dublin

Lyrath Estate Hotel

Address: Dublin Rd, Lyrath, Co. Kilkenny

The Druids Glen Hotel

Address: Leabeg Upper, Newtown Mount Kennedy, Co. Wicklow

Things to Note

Ireland uses kilometres, and N Ireland uses miles, so be aware of the changes as you cross the border. If renting, make sure your car rental insurance covers you in both countries.

If you're on a budget, avoid the M roads (motorway roads), many of which have tolls R country roads will take you through small towns and add to the distance and driving time, but this is a great way to get off the beaten track if you have time.

Tolls in Ireland range from €1.70 to €10 for a standard car. Roads are as follows:

- **M** (Motorway, some with toll charges and some without)
- **N** (National Roads, free and all in good condition)
- **R** (Regional Roads, all free, but conditions can vary, and the roads are generally narrower and windier than others, take caution)
- **A** Roads are national roads in Northern Ireland.
- **B** Roads are regional roads in N Ireland.

The Shelbourne Hotel, Co. Dublin

Dates for the Diary

- **Pancake Tuesday** - Always falls the day before Ash Wednesday and is a day the Irish love. You most certainly need to eat pancakes if you are in Ireland on this day, it's tradition.

- **The Jameson Dublin Film Festival** - Is usually held in February in Dublin

- **St Patrick's Day** - 17th March every year. There is always a celebration no matter where you are in the country, but get your spot early to watch the parade

- **Fleadh Nua Music Festival** - Held in May/June, in Ennis County Clare, the streets and pubs are filled with music

- **Galway Arts Festival** - 12th -25th July

- **Rose of Tralee** - This beauty and talent pageant is held in August each year

- **Winter Solstice** - 21st Dec, most famously viewed at Newgrange passage tomb in County Meath, but this incredibly popular event must be booked in advance.

Staying Safe

Ireland wouldn't be considered one of the most dangerous places in the world, but of course, just like anywhere, it is advisable to take the usual precautions to stay safe, to ensure you have a relaxing trip.

Over ten million tourists visit Ireland each year without any crime complaints or issues, however between the 1960s and the 1990s during the times of 'The Troubles', the country was prone to hostility, and it wasn't uncommon to hear of bombs and riots. These days, apart from some areas in certain major cities, Ireland is a much safer place to travel, and it is certainly not considered to be dangerous as a whole.

It is always important to be vigilant, so here are some of the main safety precautions we would advise for travel around Ireland.

- Do not forget that in Ireland we drive on the left hand. It is also worth noting that if you drive over the border to the

Blarney Castle, Co. Cork (commons.wikimedia.org)

93

north, you will swiftly change from kilometres to miles, so don't get caught out.

- As with most cities, it is important to be aware of possible pickpockets, especially in the centres of most major cities. It is generally safer in the countryside, but you should be streetwise wherever you go on your trip. If an area seems unsafe, even at night, it's best to move on and find an alternative spot.

- Don't flash wallets or expensive items in public, or leave valuables out of sight.

- When visiting areas such as the Cliffs of Moher, and other exposed sites, be aware that some areas are open to the cliff edge and can be extremely windy, so be cautious.

- Make sure to always lock your vehicle and do not leave valuables on display for passersby to spot.

Tips from the Locals

- To get the best experiences in Ireland try to eat, drink and visit places that the locals do, as opposed to always following the tourist route.

- Ireland is free on Wednesday: Many of Ireland's heritage sites are free of charge on the first Wednesday of every month, with over 80 places to choose from. That will keep you busy.

- Invest in a Heritage Card to get all of these heritage sites free for a whole year, when you pay a one-off fee for the card.

- Early Bird Menus are a great way to try local food without breaking the bank, so check out what offers local restaurants have as well as checking out the following *www.groupon.ie* and *www.livingsocial.ie* for great offers.

- For any extras on the road, stop at a Tesco Extra to stock up and save money. They also have laundry machines outside the supermarket, if that is on your to-do list.

- Use the Park4Night app to find places to park for free, stop overnight in your

Galway Oysters (commons.wikimedia.org)

campervan and find facilities such as water refilling, gas stations and laundry, an excellent app to have on your phone and it can be used offline for a monthly fee, which can save you data.

Download the app Maps Me to get routing options, find facilities etc. Without having to use your data. Just download the map you need as you go.

Although wild camping is allowed, always take note of any signs not allowing campervans or overnight parking and opt for an alternative spot. Also, leave nothing but footprints and take nothing but photographs when wild camping.

• Be sure to have access to an Irish calendar, so you know the major holidays, when shops and sites may be closed.

• Be sure to head to Sean's Bar in Athlone for a pint of Guinness in the oldest pub in Ireland and possibly the world.

• If you're after some live Irish music, be sure to head to Whelans in Dublin, Roisin Dubh in Galway as well as most city streets where you'll find up and coming acts busking.

• Do not greet locals with the phrase 'Top of the mornin' to ya', you may be shocked to know that nobody actually says that in Ireland. A simple hello or 'howaya' will do just fine.

• Slainte is Irish for Cheers, and people will be more than happy if you say it when out for a pint.

Now that you have made the first move to plan your Ultimate Irish Road Trip, you have plenty of choices here on what you want to see, do, eat and drink on the island. Of course, it all depends on how long

you have to spend travelling around, but we guarantee that however, many days it is, it will not be long enough. Ireland is a country like no other, an island with one of the friendliest nations in the world, a land steeped in history with endless sites to explore, and incredible scenery that will blow your mind.

You will be pleasantly surprised that for such a small country, it is jam-packed full of adventure, beauty, once in a lifetime experiences and much more, so we promise you, it will be hard to leave this place. Ireland has the perfect balance of tourist attractions which you would have heard about such as The Giant's Causeway and The Guinness Storehouse, and local

Cliffs of Moher, Co. Clare (commons.wikimedia.org)

experiences which you will encounter as you get off the beaten track, so we encourage you to lose yourself in the country's character. Be open to not having everything completely planned out, to encountering amazing adventures, meeting locals and stopping at newly discovered destinations. These are the experiences that will make your road trip in Ireland so incredibly memorable.

Be mindful to take in every moment of the journey, to sometimes only capture the views with your memory and not always your camera, to watch and listen to each wave as it crashes to the shore, each star as it sparkles in the clear skies of the countryside and each corner you turn that leads you to yet another breathtaking scene. This is the essence of Ireland, and this is what you will remember most of all as you journey through the Emerald Isle on your Ultimate Irish Road Trip.

About the Author

Jade Chantel Poleon, is a seasoned traveller and travel writer, having set off on her world travels in 2007. Since then, she has travelled to 90 countries throughout the globe, but Ireland, her homeland, remains one of her absolute favourites. She enjoys hiking, travel writing, photography, road trips, as well as having cultural experiences and loves to inspire others to travel to Ireland.

She has explored Ireland extensively but believes that you can never truly see everything it has to offer, despite the small size of the country, and each trip there is a whole new experience. One of her favourite ways to travel is to drive, and she is currently on a road trip around Europe with her dog

Gimli and her campervan, a journey she will surely continue back in her home country in the near future.

Glendalough Moutains, Co. Wicklow (commons.wikimedia.org)

Credits

Editor & Publisher - Stevie Haughey

Assistant Editor - Siân McQuillan   **Designer** - Matt Jordan

Copyright © 2022 by Ireland Before You Die

Made in the USA
Monee, IL
13 February 2023

27644673R00056